TEETH ON EDGE

TEETH ON EDGE

Robert O. Fife

BAKER BOOK HOUSE
Grand Rapids, Michigan

Printed in the United States of America

To Wayne and Kathy
Who Are Part of
the Solution

PREFACE

If the church of Jesus is to honor its commitment to His ministry of reconciliation it must come to grips with racism — that powerful, insidious form of human alienation. As the Community of Ultimate Concern, the church dare not close its eyes to the agony of a generation caught in the conflict of passion and prejudice.

But if it is to serve men effectively in Jesus' name, the church must embody His will in its own life. Only in this way can it demonstrate what the kingdom of God is.

Yet, all too often the church has passively reflected the spirit of the age, and the radical call to repentance has been muted or utterly silenced. Perhaps nowhere has this failure been more evident than in the church's response to the contemporary racial crisis.

How are men to find their way amidst the confusion of such a time? The road is difficult and complex, but it is marked by four signposts: Concern; Understanding; Resolution; Solution. Although the scene is rapidly changing, the author hopes that this work will serve the reader's pilgrimage along the way.

It is impossible to express adequately one's debt to others in such an endeavor. Prof. Dean E. Walker, Prof. John D. Barnhart, and W. Carl Ketcherside were sources of encouragement. Invaluable assistance in utilizing original sources was afforded by librarians of Lexington Theological Seminary, Christian Theological Seminary, Indiana University, Elon College, Atlantic Christian College, the Huntington Library, and the Manuscript Division of the Library of

Congress. The resources of the Disciples of Christ Historical Society were also of great help.

Faculty colleagues of Milligan College and of Pepperdine University, where the author spent a gratifying year as a Visiting Professor, have offered many helpful suggestions. New vistas in social ethics were opened through studies as a Fellow by Courtesy in the University of Southern California. A special word of appreciation is due those Black friends, notably Calvin Bowers, Dean of Pepperdine Ethnic Studies Department, whose earnest interest provided exciting stimulation for the task.

Finally, to my family, which participated in this experience in a very meaningful way, I can only express loving gratitude.

Milligan College, Tennessee
1971

CONTENTS

Preface

I

A SCIENTIFIC AGE

CONFRONTS A PROPHETIC JUDGMENT

Multitudes, multitudes in the valley of decision! for the day of Jehovah is near in the valley of decision.

— JOEL 3:14, ASV

The racist white Christian church with its hypocritical declarations and doctrines of brotherhood has abused our trust and faith.

— THE BLACK MANIFESTO (1969)

How did it happen that at the very moment men first stood on the moon, mobs of the discontented on "the beautiful earth" were burning their own cities? What is the nature of this paradox of modern man? Is it not ironical that a society whose law and tradition guarantee to every person the dignity of equity and justice should be rejected by many of its citizens in the name of freedom? Why are the religious institutions which affirm brotherhood scorned by many whose ethical judgments stem from the very heritage they reject?

It is a serious fact that man's technical "know-how" has run far ahead of his ethical and moral achievements.[1] Perhaps this gap has never been so great as now. How wide can it become before our very humanity is strained to the

---

[1]Arnold Toynbee has written, "The significance of a landing on the moon lies in its forcing us to face — and, we may hope, to deal effectively with — the ludicrous, but also perilous, discrepancy between our attainments in technology and in morals." "What It Could Mean," *New York Post*, July 19, 1969. Quoted in *Current*, September, 1969, p. 5.

11

breaking point? How long can civilization survive the vast
expansion of its technology and the gross neglect of human
brotherhood?

A society must be bound together by some commonly accepted sense of identity. Unless a people *think* of themselves
as a people, they face social disintegration. Yet, it is this
very fate which threatens western civilization.

Societies have differed throughout history in the centers
of identity around which they have formed. In some, the
tribal or blood relationship has been the cohesive factor.
In Greece, it was the concept of the city state. Romans
thought in terms of citizenship in the Empire. Medieval
Europeans were loosely united in a sense of Christendom.

The rise of nationalism and of the Protestant Reformation
shattered the unity of Christendom. Wars of religion gave
way to conflicts between nation states. The democracies of
the West came to define the nation in *constitutional* terms.
This meant that people of various cultures, religions, and
races could belong to one nation through common allegiance
to one body of law.

Karl Marx sought to replace all of these forms of social
identity with that of social class. "Working-men of all countries, unite!" was the call of the *Communist Manifesto*.
Marx saw the working classes of every race or nation locked
in mortal combat with "bourgeois society." Therefore,
workers ought to unite across national or racial lines to
destroy the other classes. "Proletarians" had "nothing to
lose but their chains."

But Marxism has not been able to overcome nationalism.
The last great World Wars were conflicts between nation
states — not between social classes. Even now, the unity of
the Communist world is shattered upon the shoals of nationalism.

The present Sino-Russian conflict is especially significant
because it has both national and racial overtones. Mao's
effort to lead a non-white Communist movement has been
violently denounced by Moscow because it differentiates

men by race as well as by social class. But even though it is un-Marxist, it has been heard in the nonwhite world.

It remained for the evil genius of Hitler to combine in one powerful system the sense of nationalism and the sense of race. The "Twenty-Five Points" of the Nazi Party declared in 1920 that only persons of "German" blood could be citizens of the German state. "No Jew," it declared, "may be a member of the nation." The racist doctrines of Houston Stewart Chamberlain were borrowed by Hitler when he formulated in *Mein Kampf* the Nazi philosophy of the "folk state."

The American Negro intellecutal, W. E. B. DuBois, spoke prophetically when he declared at the turn of the century, "The problem of the twentieth century is the problem of the color line."[2] DuBois could hardly have anticipated the racism of Hitler Germany in which millions were incinerated even though they were of the same "color" as "Aryans." Nonetheless, the insight may well be true. Future historians may simply state, "The problem of the twentieth century was the problem of race." Certainly, an increasing number of the peoples of the world are thinking of themselves *first* in terms of their racial identity. If this trend continues, the results will be incalculable.

But if the rising tide of racism challenges both democratic and communist nationalism, it challenges yet more critically the universal spirit of the Christian faith. Perhaps this is not altogether unexpected, for the church's mission in the world associates it in the minds of many with the patterns of the age. This is nowhere more clearly seen than in the concurrence of the missionary thrust of the church with western military and economic expansion.[3]

The simple formula, "To Christianize is to Westernize," was perhaps not consciously espoused by missionaries, but

---

[2]This was the thesis of his influential book, *The Souls of Black Folk* (Greenwich: Fawcett Publications, Inc., 1961).

[3]Even the great missionary David Livingstone became increasingly drawn into "imperial" affairs in the course of his African sojourn.

it was, nonetheless, the end result of much of their endeavors. The expediencies of western expansionism, such as the Kiachow incident or the Boxer uprising,[4] made it appear to many non-westerners that the Christian faith was but the religious arm of western colonial power. Little wonder that the anticolonial movement following World War II should be accompanied in many places by an anti-Christian counterpart.

All of this has not been lost upon American Negroes. A distinct line of descent may be traced from David Walker's *Appeal to the Colored Citizens of the World* (1829) through the writing of Marcus Garvey at the turn of the century, and into the present with its Black Muslims and Black Panthers. It is not accidental that amidst this rising tide of Black awareness the charge should be made that the "American Christ, with his blue eyes and blond hair" is a "white man's Jesus"; the espousal of His religion has been the white man's way of enslaving the Black; the black man's freedom will never be attained through devotion to the white man's Jesus; the black man needs his own religion.[5]

This attack upon Christianity as the white man's religion presents the black Christian especially with a burden difficult to bear. He is subjected to attack as a "lackey" or an "Uncle Tom" because of his devotion to Christ, and his refusal to turn upon his white Christian brother.[6] Yet these very "white brothers," while confessing the Negroes' equality before God, have often refused to treat them as equals before

---

[4]For a good discussion of these events see Kenneth S. Latourette, *The Chinese: Their History and Culture* (New York: Macmillan, 4th ed., 1964), pp. 309, 315-317 respectively.

[5]See "Interview with an Arsonist," in Ben W. Gilbert, *et al., Ten Blocks From The White House* (New York: Praeger, 1968), p. 159; also "Black Power and the American Christ," in Floyd B. Barbour, *The Black Power Revolt* (Boston: Porter Sargent, 1968), p. 87. See also *The Black Manifesto*.

[6]Robert F. Williams quotes a prominent minister in South Carolina as saying, "Our biggest stumbling block is the Uncle Tom minister — the people must stop paying these traitors." *Negroes with Guns*, quoted in Barbour, *op. cit.*, p. 151.

men. An increasing number of younger black Americans are consequently being alienated from Christianity.

Therefore, we must look at race, and ultimately to the problem of race as it reflects upon the nature of the church. First, however, a number of observations need to be made.

It is important to distinguish between the *fact* of race, and the *problem* of race. The fact of race is genetic and natural. Nature knows no racial "problem." The problem of race is social and spiritual. The problem may be *occasioned* by the genetics of racial differences, but it is not *caused* by it. The cause of racism is of a different order.

Racism is a dimension of human sin. Where man's alienation from his fellow has at times centered upon local, tribal, religious or national differences, *racism is the focus of human alienation on racial differences*. But the alienation is originally neither genetic nor social. It is fundamentally a spiritual problem. The Bible sees it as man's projection upon his brother of his own alienation from God.

Racism will never be adequately understood apart from this theological dimension. Sociology informs our understanding as it speaks to the problems of "social density," "social distance," "de-facto segregation," or "blockbusting." Psychology provides insight into the effect of these social situations in producing a definable "disadvantaged American Negro personality." It speaks of "oppression psychosis," "exaggerated aggression," or "playing Negro."[7]

All of these insights are invaluable to an understanding of the problem of racism, but in themselves they do not explain the fundamental "Why?" For all its contributions, a purely scientific approach to the problem of race is insufficient, because the problem is not altogether subject to scientific methodology. The problem is ultimately one of the

---

[7]See Aaron L. Rutledge and Gertrude Z. Gass, *Nineteen Negro Men* (San Francisco: Jossey-Bass, 1968), pp. 44, 45; also, "Power, Personality, and Protest," in Charles E. Silberman, *Crisis in Black and White* (New York: Vintage Books, 1964), p. 189 f.

human heart, and ultimately the solution must speak to the heart of man.[8]

It is difficult even to describe (to say nothing of analyze) the contemporary racial problem in the United States. That it is part of a rising sense of racism throughout the world we have already noted. But the pattern becomes exceedingly complex in America. How can one accurately measure the growing sense of racial awareness in this country? It pervades the thinking of the whole populace in ways both subtle and overt. Even those who most wish it otherwise find themselves subconsciously thinking in racial terms.

The economic and social facts of life are patent for all to see. The nonwhite portion of the population has a much lower standard of living; occupies inferior housing; has fewer opportunities for employment; is more limited in education; is culturally differentiated in manner of speech, musical tastes, and forms of religious expression.[9]

But these social phenomena which are statistically verifiable reveal strong currents which operate beneath the surface of American cultural life. These have to do with the informal, unwritten *attitudes* of the time. How does one express statistically the sense of disillusionment which pervades much of the Negro community? How is one accurately to measure the feeling generated by the assassination of

---

[8]Eugene Rabinowitch has written, "Of course, many — perhaps the most important — social challenges of our time are such that science and technology cannot contribute decisively to answering them." "From Alamogordo to Apollo: Will Man Heed the Lesson?" *Bulletin of the Atomic Scientists*, September 1969. Reprinted by permission of Science and Public Affairs, the *Bulletin of the Atomic Scientists*. Copyright 1970 by the Educational Foundation for Nuclear Science.

The optimism with which certain members of the scientific community view the possibility of solving the "human predicament" by programing genetic changes leaves the fundamental question unanswered: "Who is to determine such a 'program,' and what criteria are to be used?"

[9]See Silberman, *op. cit.*, p. 235 f.; also E. Franklin Frazier, *The Negro in the United States* (New York: Macmillan, 1967), chapter XXIII.

Martin Luther King or Malcolm X? Where are the criteria by which disillusionment with the rule of law is to be evaluated? Obviously, what data is available can only be assessed by insight (*Verstehen*, the sociologist would call it), for these massive problems defy adequate measurement.

It is difficult for those who are relatively untouched by the problem of race to appreciate its power and complexity. It has always seemed "easy" for those far removed from social problems to provide "expert" advice concerning solutions. But it is also difficult for those who are caught up in such struggles to understand them. Where the man at a distance lacks the *involvement* necessary to understanding, the man who is involved has difficulty achieving the *perspective* necessary to understanding. It is to be hoped that a measure of insight may come as a result of this excursion into the past — that perhaps a review of how things came to be the way they are may cast some light upon the way out of this agonizing "American Dilemma."[10]

While the world is becoming increasingly race conscious, America's problem is magnified by the fact that slavery rests at the root of white-Negro relations. The United States is a nation of immigrants, most of whom came of their own volition in quest of a better life. But the American Negro is a descendant of "forced immigrants" for whom a "better life" was hardly a "live option." This fact makes their position and role in American life different from that of any other immigrant group. It also makes race relations in the United States peculiarly difficult, fixing upon it a "mark of Cain" which is difficult to erase.

Perhaps it is because of this heritage the Negro is commonly considered inferior by descendents of other immigrant groups. (Witness the New York Jewish cab driver who boasts, "There never has been, and never will be, a Nigger in this cab.") Yet, the ancestors of the Jewish cabbie were

---

[10]This is, of course, the title of a classic study of the American racial problem by the famous Swedish sociologist, Gunnar Myrdal.

themselves once slaves. What, then, is the difference? The
Jew has a heritage of liberation in the memory of which
he finds identity, but *the Negro has suffered the loss of his
cultural continuity*. The significance of this fact can hardly
be overestimated. It is at the root of the contemporary
Negro quest of identity.

Just as an individual who suffers from amnesia does not
know who he is, a people without history cannot know themselves. This is one of the abiding consequences of the
slavery system. *The slave trade broke the cultural continuity of the African*. Presumably, the slave was to be acculturated to western white ways, but even this was of necessity limited by the nature of the situation.[11]

When antislavery sentiment became sufficiently strong in
the early days of the Republic to lead to passage of an act
forbidding the importation of slaves after 1808, it was believed that slavery would wither away within the United
States. However, those entertaining this fond expectation
were doomed to disappointment. The demand for slave labor was to increase with the opening up of lands in the
southern Mississippi Valley, and this led to the most nefarious commerce of all — "slave breeding." States of the upper South, whose soil was exhausted by years of wasteful
agriculture were to find an outlet for surplus slaves or those
who were troublesome, by "selling them down the river."
It is significant that even yet the phrase, "sold down the
river," carries overtones of injustice. The original practice,
often involving separation of families, was a gross betrayal
of humanity itself.

Adjustment to the culture of the white world was limited
not only by the slaves' own capacities, but also by the ex-
igencies of slavery itself. The exponents of slavery did not
want the slave to become fully acculturated, as for example,

---

[11]Frantz Fanon observed, "Without a Negro past, without a Negro
future, it was impossible for me to live my Negrohood. Not yet
white, no longer wholly black, I was damned." Quoted in Barbour,
op. cit., p. 130.

to learn to read. Were he to become literate, the slave might become dissatisfied with bondage.[12] This was, of course, a true insight. There is a distinct connection between the revolts of Denmark Vesey and Nat Turner (both of whom could read), and the laws restricting education of slaves.

Many white persons are unaware of the significance which this interdiction of Negro culture has for the contemporary Afro-American's quest of identity. The Irish enjoy St. Patrick's Day, the Scots thrill to the bagpipes. The Jewish community finds fulfillment in observance of Passover, and Orientals continue to retain their rich cultural heritage. Yet, the Negro looks back through his undoubted cultural contributions such as jazz and the spiritual and comes to the blank wall of slavery. Neither he, nor the average white American, has any conception of the cultural attainments of African civilizations such as those of the Sudan or of Ghana.[13]

It ought not be surprising, therefore, that in a day of rising racial awareness the Negro community should seek reconstruction of its ethnic continuity. This is in part accomplished through solid historical study. But where facts fail, myth is available. Man has long been a "mythmaker," using highly symbolic forms to express historical truth, or to embody his self-understanding. Speaking to the National Conference on Black Power, Adelaide Cromwell Hill said:

> We can say, and with some documentation to substantiate it, that our slave forebears could have been kings or prophets or farmers or fishermen from Ni-

---

[12]Tocqueville astutely observed in 1837, that where the ancients used fetters of iron to maintain slavery, the Americans in their system of slavery "employed their despotism and their violence against the human mind." The result was to deprive the slave "even of his desire for freedom." Quoted in Silberman, *op. cit.,* p. 79. See also Winthrop D. Jordan's discussion of "The Chain of Being" in *White Over Black* (Baltimore: Penguin, 1969), p. 482 f.

[13]An excellent survey of African cultural development may be found in Silberman, *op. cit.,* p. 162 f. See also Paul Bohannan, *Africa and the Africans* (New York: Doubleday, 1964).

geria or from Ghana, from Mozambique or from
Kenya. And for the purposes of identity, it does not
make much difference which group we choose —
they were all black, and they all came from Africa.[14]

The quest of identity is a quest of pride. It roots in rejection of the notion that in order to be worthy of respect the American Negro must "pass" into the white world. It repudiates the long-standing and deep-rooted tendency to measure the elevation of the Black according to the degree to which he straightens his hair, and cultivates the tastes of the white American. Many feel that having been refused "integration" into the mainstream of American life the alternative is separation and the cultivation of an Afro-American ethos which can provide a sense of identity and of worth.

It is necessary to recognize that the Negro community is divided over this issue.[15] Many Blacks have achieved constructive places within society and are making significant contributions to American culture.

But to an increasing number of extremists these Negroes are "Uncle Toms." They are not true "Blacks" (and the difference between "Negro" and "Black" is to some significant). They have been "brainwashed" by "Whitey," and have lost their integrity. To whom the future of the Negro-Black community belongs is a real question at this point.

The church is judged by the racial crisis of America. It is judged because it bears a Gospel for all men, and it is called by its Lord to be a universal brotherhood. Yet, it has been caught within the web of social circumstance to the extent

---

[14]"What is Africa to Us?" in Barbour, *op. cit.*, p. 134.

[15]Lawrence P. Neal has written, "Psychologically, Black America is divided between itself as a separate nation and seeing itself as an integral part of American society." "Black Power in the International Context," in Barbour, *op. cit.*, p. 138. See also Harold Cruse, *The Crisis of the Negro Intellectual* (New York: William Morrow, 1967), p. 421 f. For an astute theological exposition of "Black Power" see James H. Cone, *Black Theology and Black Power* (New York: The Seabury Press, 1969).

that the universal Gospel and the universal fellowship have been seriously compromised.

Instead of judging the social order, and challenging men to repentance and reformation, the church has all too readily allowed the social order to determine the message it should proclaim and the way of life it should exemplify.[16] This tendency has long been recognized in the relation which social class bears to the rise of denominationalism.[17] It remains for American churches to consider seriously the meaning of their ready acceptance of restrictive racial patterns in light of the Gospel of reconciliation.

One of the most serious judgments to be made upon the American church is that it has obscured the true Christ, the Son of Man. Perhaps this charge is not altogether justified, but the church cannot escape a share of the responsibility for the rejection of Christ by many who are genuinely concerned. One black Christian writing of the flight of the middle class churches to the suburbs, says, "This very exodus of the Christians from the places where the weak and powerless live has been one of the primary motivating forces of Black Power."[18]

While the middle classes have as much need of the Gospel as the poor, the flight of many churches to the suburbs is actually a new form of monasticism. The critical problems of the inner city may be left behind. Missionary endeavor in distant places can occupy the energy and strength of congregations in "a good cause," with the result that little time or few resources remain to be devoted to the plight of those nearby. The words of Jesus are here appropriate: ". . .These ye ought to have done, and not to have left the other undone" (Matt. 23:23, ASV).

---

[16]Peter L. Berger, *The Noise of Solemn Assemblies: Christian Commitment and the Religious Establishment In America* (Garden City: Doubleday, 1961).

[17]H. Richard Niebuhr, *Social Sources of Denominationalism* (Reprinted, Magnolia, Mass.: Peter Smith).

[18]Vincent Harding, "Black Power and the American Christ," in Barbour, *op. cit.,* p. 88.

Another option chosen by some is the acceptance of the philosophy of the "secular city,"[19] in which the church is absorbed into the "city of man." Indeed, it is commonplace in some quarters to hear all forms of religious institutions condemned as part of the "white power establishment." Even the rightful existence of congregations has been challenged.

The concerned Christian who does not find in either the new monasticism or the new secularism a viable alternative must still recognize that the church remains under the judgment of the Word of God. The church is heir to a prophetic tradition which both *forthtells* and *foretells,* and *it behooves the church to hear that prophetic word.*

The prophetic forthtelling declares the "sure Word of God" in the human situation. "But let justice roll down as waters, and righteousness as a mighty stream," it thunders (Amos 5:24, ASV). Or, it asks the pertinent question, ". . . What doth Jehovah require of thee, but to do justly, and to love kindness, and to walk humbly with thy God?" (Mic. 6: 8, ASV).

The prophetic foretelling is not arbitrary prediction. Neither is it some declaration of an inevitable Fate. Prophetic foretelling is rooted in God's sovereign quest of man's participation in His providence. It *links the course of history to ethical decision.* God visits His people in revelation to inform them of His will (Luke 1:68, 78), and He visits them to execute judgment in light of their decisions (Hos. 9:7; Mic. 7:4). So Jesus wept over Jerusalem because its inhabitants did not recognize their "day of visitation" (Luke 19:44). Israel had made a spiritual decision — rejection of the Messiah — and would suffer, therefore, the historical consequences which Jesus foretold.

When one views the present racial crisis from within the prophetic tradition he may well hear the ancient proverb echo out of the past: ". . . THE FATHERS HAVE EATEN

---

[19]Harvey Cox, *The Secular City* (New York: Macmillan, 1965).

SOUR GRAPES, AND THE CHILDREN'S TEETH ARE SET ON EDGE" (Jer. 31:29; Ezek. 18:2).

In the light of this prophetic judgment, what is the church to do in the present? The church must understand anew the declaration of the Gospel that because of the Cross, "There can be neither Jew nor Greek, there can be neither bond nor free, there can be no male and female; for ye all are one *man* in Christ Jesus" (Gal. 3:28, ASV; see also Col. 3:11).

The church must examine afresh what is incumbent upon it as the community of the servants of God. How is it properly to relate itself and the Gospel it bears to the social order? How do the distinctions inherent in the social order relate to the one fellowship which is entered through baptism and renewed at the Table of the Lord? What are the contemporary obligations of love to one's neighbor as unto oneself?

What are the Biblical implications of the racial segregation of the churches? How is the church to minister to the needs of both whites and Blacks, caught up in the spirit of alienation? Is it true that the church participated in the enslavement of the Negro?

Answers to these questions require perspective. The teeth of this generation are, indeed, set on edge. Only as we understand the nature of the bitter fruit of which our fathers partook may we understand the way to peace and reconciliation.

If we can appreciate the complexities and difficulties which our fathers faced, both slave and free, we may be more patient in resolution of our own.

But above all, if we can discern in the present tragic crisis the authentication of the prophetic insight that the course of history is, indeed, linked to spiritual decision, we may be prepared for the sake of our children's children to break the fateful sequence of bitter fruit by a decisive act of justice, reconciliation, and charity.

II

MUTUAL BONDAGE:

THE SOCIAL SETTING OF SLAVERY

. . . Father, forgive them; for they know not what they do . . .
— LUKE 23:34, ASV

When one views the system of slavery after having made
an attempt to get "within an understanding distance" of it,
he may well conclude that it was in a very real sense a system of *mutual bondage*. While the Negro was held in bondage of a very clear and obvious nature, the white master was
bound with him by a yoke equally real although, perhaps,
less obvious.

Let us first consider the system as it affected *Slaves of
Masters*.

The slave trade had become a well-marked system by the
advent of the nineteenth century.[1] African traders purchased slaves from tribal chiefs and other Blacks who
profited from the sale of their fellows. These were brought
to the coast where they were in turn purchased by captains
of slave ships and transported under the most inhuman conditions to the Caribbean.

The slave trade was triangular in nature. Having brought
slaves to the Caribbean, the captains would sell them for
sugar or molasses. Transporting their cargo to New England
they would exchange it for rum. The rum was highly prized

---

[1] A classic work describing the slave trade is William E. B. DuBois,
Suppression of the African Slave Trade . . . 1638-1870 (New York,
1896). See also Basil Davidson, et al., *A History of West Africa*
(Garden City: Doubleday, 1966). See also Philip D. Curtin, *The
Atlantic Slave Trade* (Madison: University of Wisconsin, 1969).

on the African coast, where it was exchanged for slaves.

After a period of acclimation and acculturation in the Caribbean Islands, the slaves would be sold to the mainland. Students of the trade have noted the distinctions which were made between slaves of the various tribes, some being better suited to certain forms of labor than others.

The obvious brutality of the system was not lost on many people of humanitarian sensitivity. The crowded slave ships were stinking death traps. The indignity of the slave market, and the sundering of human relationships which took place there were common, but nonetheless tragic, aspects of the system.

The blighting effect of slavery burdened those who took time to think. They could see that it was not in keeping with the free institutions of the new Republic. Neither was it a sound basis of economy. This is to say nothing of the offence which slavery gave to the religious convictions of many. For these reasons, antislavery sentiment was to be found very early in both North and South.

There are numerous signs of the hopeful concern with which slavery was viewed at the opening of the nineteenth century. George Washington and John Randolph of Roanoke emancipated their servants by will.[2] Jefferson, Madison, and Patrick Henry were but a few of the eminent leaders who opposed the slave trade.[3] Many thought the law forbidding importation of slaves after 1808 would be but a first step toward the ultimate abolition of the system.[4]

---

[2]*The Writings of George Washington,* ed. by John C. Fitzpatrick (39 vols., Washington, 1931-1944), XXXVII, pp. 276, 359; Hugh A. Garland, *Life of John Randolph of Roanoke* (New York, 13th ed., 1890), p. 372.

[3]*The Writings of Thomas Jefferson,* ed. by Paul L. Ford (10 vols. New York, 1892, I, 28; Sidney H. Gay, *James Madison* (New York, 1884), pp. 320, 321; Moses G. Tyler, *Patrick Henry* (New York, 1887), pp. 388, 389.

[4]For these proceedings see James D. Richardson, *Messages and Papers of the Presidents, 1789-1897* (10 vols., Washington, 1907), II, pp. 63, 95; *Annals of Congress,* XXXVI, XXXVII. See also DuBois, *Suppression of the African Slave Trade,* p. 94.

Concurrent with the laws prohibiting further importation of slaves, manumission societies were formed throughout the new country. The first of these had been established in Philadelphia in 1774 under the presidency of Benjamin Franklin. A New York society was headed by John Jay and Alexander Hamilton. Similar organizations were formed in Delaware, Rhode Island, Connecticut, New Jersey, Virginia, and Maryland.[5] The "Tennessee Society for Promoting the Manumission of Slaves" was formed in 1815. By 1827 there were 106 antislavery societies in the South, with over five thousand members.[6]

Not being protected from the slavery system by a federal statute, as was the old Northwest under the Ordinance of 1787,[7] the antislavery forces in the South had to wage their struggle state by state.

In 1819 Elihu Embree first published *The Emancipator* in Jonesboro, Tennessee. Indicative of the interest in his cause is the fact that within a year it had two thousand subscribers.[8]

David Rice, "father of Presbyterianism in Kentucky," led an antislavery movement in the Kentucky Constitutional Convention of 1792.[9] A later critical constitutional battle developed with David Purviance, a Christian minister, leading a campaign for gradual emancipation against the "slaveocracy"

---

[5]Merrill Jensen, *The New Nation* (New York, 1950), p. 135.

[6]Chase C. Mooney, *Slavery in Tennessee* (Bloomington, Ind., 1957), pp. 65, 66; also Asa E. Martin, "The Anti-Slavery Societies of Tennessee," *Tennessee Historical Magazine*, I (1915), pp. 261-280.

[7]The Sixth Article of this Ordinance provided that there should be "neither slavery nor involuntary servitude in the said territory, otherwise than in punishment of crimes whereof the party shall have been duly convicted." *The Territorial Papers of the United States,* ed. by Clarence E. Carter (Washington, 1934), I, p. 49.

[8]*The Emancipator,* ed. by Elihu Embree (Jonesborough, Tenn., 1820; Reprinted, Nashville, 1932).

[9]John D. Barnhart, *Valley of Democracy* (Bloomington, Ind., 1953), p. 91 f.; William E. Connelley and E. Merton Coulter, *History of Kentucky* (5 vols., Chicago, 1922), I, p. 283.

headed by John Breckinridge.[10]

In 1796, and again in 1834, Tennessee constitutional conventions witnessed strong attempts to make slavery illegal in that state.[11]

Meanwhile, in the Virginia Constitutional Convention of 1832, Alexander Campbell led western delegates in a struggle to implement gradual emancipation in that state. Campbell actually suggested a plan for the reimbursement of slaveowners and for the rehabilitation of their freed slaves. His efforts were sufficiently noteworthy to gain the admiration of Madison, but failed of passage. Caleb Upshur stated the slaveowners' position clearly when he said, "Property is entitled to protection, and . . . *our* property imperiously demands *that kind of protection* which flows from the possession of power."[12]

For his part, Campbell replied:

> If we exhaust our energies on these little localities, time, the great innovator, will break our arrangements to pieces: For it is decreed, that every system of Government not based upon the true philosophy of man — not adapted to public opinion, to the genius of the age, shall fall into ruins.[13]

In none of these efforts were antislavery forces successful. While many did not abandon hope, there commenced a steady emigration of people of antislavery views out of the South, most of them moving into the Old Northwest. Typi-

---

[10]Connelley and Coulter, *op. cit.*, I, pp. 315; 540; Levi Purviance, *The Biography of Elder David Purviance* (Dayton, O., 1848), pp. 11-17.

[11]Chase C. Mooney, "The Question of Slavery and the Free Negro in the Tennessee Constitutional Convention of 1834," *Journal of Southern History*, XII (1946), p. 489.

[12]*Proceedings and Debates of the Virginia Constitutional Convention of 1829-1830* (Richmond, 1830), p. 83. Hereafter designated *Virginia Proceedings*. See also, Harold L. Lunger, *The Political Ethics of Alexander Campbell* (St. Louis, 1954), p. 75 f.

[13]*Virginia Proceedings*, p. 390.

cal of these was Purviance, who moved to Ohio in 1807, there to participate in the legislature, and to serve as president of the Board of Trustees of Miami University. Whole congregations moved into the free territory as, for example, the Quakers who settled in Plainfield, Indiana.

In the course of this exodus the South lost many gifted people whose emigration seriously weakened the cause of emancipation. At the same time, the hold of slavery was further strengthened by development of certain economic factors. The invention of the cotton gin, the cultivation of new strains of cotton, and the opening of the Mississippi basin, provided a tremendous demand for labor — and slave labor was more readily available than free.[14]

Thus the South moved over a watershed which is clearly perceptible from this distance.

But the failure of emancipation was not only occasioned by the supposed value of slave labor. The prospect of a large body of Negro freemen confronted the white citizenry with a dilemma. If the slaves were emancipated, they must be accepted as equals under the law, or kept in a separate society. Simple emancipation would call for the first alternative. But since a large number of whites did not welcome this prospect, simple emancipation had been largely abandoned. In its stead an alternative plan of "colonization" was proposed. Emancipation was, in this view, only a prelude to the emigration of Negroes back to Africa. The contemporary relevance of these alternatives is seen in the controversy between integrationists and separatists.

The American Colonization Society was founded in 1817. It early enjoyed the support of a number of eminent men, including Bushrod Washington, nephew of the first presi-

---

[14]See J. D. Hill, "Economic Aspects of Slavery," *South Atlantic Quarterly,* XXVI (1927), p. 161; William H. Yarbrough, *Economic Aspects of Slavery in Relation to Southern and Southwestern Migration* (Nashville, 1932), p. 8 f.; Lewis C. Gray, *Agriculture in the Southern United States to 1860* (2 vols., Washington, 1933).

dent, James Madison, James Monroe, and John Marshall
— all of whom served as presidents of the Society.[15]

Although these men opposed slavery, they did not see
simple emancipation as providing a viable "solution." The
plight of Negroes already free was hardly a promising
foretaste of universal emancipation. Neither did white society appear ready to grant them the opportunities necessary to self-improvement. Since some whites were offended
by slavery while others were fearful of a large population of
free Negroes, the Colonization Society was developed as a
sort of "third option."

R. R. Gurley, secretary of the Society reflected these
views when he said that the 250,000 "free people of colour"
were only "nominally free." They had "few means or mo-
tives for improvement," and were forced to live in circumstances which practically forbade "higher qualities of character." Since he did not see that the circumstances of free
Negroes were likely to change, Gurley thought their removal to Africa would be a blessing to all.[16]

The emigration of freedmen to Africa would, in the
judgment of supporters of colonization, achieve two major
goals: First, it would do away with the evils of slavery.
Second, it would "save" American society from large numbers of free Negroes whose presence was not viewed with
optimism by the colonizationists.

The program of the Society was to sponsor the emancipation of slaves, their education, and their consequent trans-
portation and settlement in the land of their ancestors. In
1821 the Society purchased land in West Africa to provide
a homeland for freedmen. It is as a result of these labors
that the Republic of Liberia was born.[17]

---

[15]Early Lee Fox, *American Colonization Society, 1817-1840. Johns
Hopkins University Studies in Historical and Political Science,*
XXXVII, no. 3 (Baltimore, 1919).

[16]Letter to Barton W. Stone, ed., *Christian Messenger* (Georgetown,
Kentucky; Jacksonville, Illinois, 1826-1845), II (1827), p. 197.

[17]Charles H. Huberich, *Political and Legislative History of Liberia*
(2 vols., New York, 1947), p. 18 f.

In spite of its eminent leadership, however, the Colonization Society faced opposition, both from slaveowners and from abolitionists. Some slaveowners welcomed it as removing Negro freedmen from positions in society where they could influence slaves. But others opposed it on the ground that it made slaves restless with their lot, constantly holding before them the possibility of freedom.

Seeking to reassure slaveowners, Henry A. Wise wrote:

> The Tennessee Colonization Society . . . looks upon the cause of colonization as peculiarly a *Southern* cause: — upon colonization societies as handmaids of the slaveholder, *not as opposed to his interests* . . . Moreover, *slave holders* desire that "free people of color" should be removed *far out of* our country — with an *ocean* between their influence and the slaves, and to a country which God and nature seem to have designed for them and for which they seem to have been formed.[18]

This type of concession to the slaveholder and his interests contributed to the charge openly expressed by some emancipationists that the Colonization Society was a "front" for the slave power. Others saw it as an inadequate half-measure, and that it was basically rooted in prejudice against the free Negro. John Fee, founder of Berea College, put it plainly: "*Prejudice,* unholy prejudice," is "at the bottom of the colonization movement."[19] If fear of the influence which a large number of free Negroes might have upon American white society is prejudice, then Fee was correct.

Fee felt it was fundamentally unjust to require a slave — or any man — to "leave the land of his birth" as a condition of freedom. It is of interest that he thought of the slave as an *American,* having attachments to this land as the land of his birth. The colonizationists presented *Africa* as the home-

---

[18]Papers, American Colonization Society (Mss. Div., Library of Congress), No. 3499, January 9, 1830.

[19]*Anti-Slavery Manual: Or, the Wrong of American Slavery Exposed by the Light of the Bible and of Facts: With a Remedy for the Evil* (Maysville, Kentucky, 1848), pp. 170-173.

land of the Negro. These alternative viewpoints sound strangely contemporary.

Elder John Rogers, carried away with his own eloquence, said that white men "would sicken and die victims of that ardent climate," while "the native African, invigorated under the influence of a vertical sun, glories in its blazes, and grapples with the lion of the desert."[20] If Africa were the true home of the Negro it was not unjust to free him in order to return.

To abolitionists such as John Fee the program of colonization actually served to fasten slavery upon the remainder of Negroes yet in bondage. If large numbers were emancipated and returned to Africa, the labor of those yet slaves would become more valuable. This would encourage the further development of the "nefarious practice" of "slave-breeding."

But other Christian leaders supported colonization for missionary reasons. It was believed that if educated and converted freedmen were settled in Africa to develop a land of their own, their influence throughout that continent could be immeasurable. "The sound of Christian instruction and Christian worship" would be heard in the "land of brooding Pagan darkness." The new colony could become "a new Christian Empire," and the freedmen would be both "happy themselves, and the instruments of happiness to others."[21]

It was in keeping with this conviction that the second missionary sent forth by the American Christian Missionary Society was Alexander Cross — a former slave who had been emancipated, educated, and sponsored by the Christian Church in Hopkinsville, Kentucky. Contrary to John Rogers' assertion that the Negro was peculiarly suited to life in Africa, Cross fell victim to a fever and died soon after his arrival in Liberia.[22]

---

[20]*Christian Messenger*, IV (1829), p. 59.

[21]*Christian Messenger*, IV (1829), pp. 59, 60.

[22]*Minutes of American Christian Missionary Society Anniversary, 1853* (n.p.), pp. 29, 230 f.

Whether former slaves could become constructive participants in American society was vigorously debated in the days of the Colonization Society. Those who pointed to the degradation common to the slave as somehow inherent in Negro nature were confirmed in the "wisdom" of colonization. On the other hand, many saw the wretchedness of Negroes, both slave and free, as a result of slavery itself. To them colonization was an unjust and prejudicial system. Their removal to Africa was a gross perversion of human rights. The solution was to follow the Biblical injunction to render unto them "that which was just and equal."

In this view, the solution to the "Negro problem" was not some plan of *colonization,* but adequate *education.* Free Negroes, said John Fee, did not constitute an insurmountable problem to white society. They were "as civil, as law-abiding, and virtuous, as any other people *with the same amount of education.*" If slaves were freed, treated as human beings, granted opportunity for education, they would develop "character" and be "safe for society."[23]

As matters developed, the Colonization Society's program, while it was responsible for the establishment of the Republic of Liberia, did not achieve its main goal — the emancipation of American slaves and their return to Africa. The reasons for this failure were obvious. In the first place, the Society did not achieve the support necessary to its program. Second, the Negro birth rate far outstripped the numbers being colonized. In its first twenty-five years, the Society colonized 4,168 emancipated slaves. During this period John Fee estimated the Negro population was increasing about 90,000 annually.[24]

In spite of its statistical failure, and the ambivalence of its program, colonization represented a very contemporary issue — also fraught with ambiguities — the rising awareness of Africa on the part of American Negroes. Some moderns

---

[23] *Anti-Slavery Manual,* pp. 173, 155.
[24] *Ibid.,* pp. 171, 172.

of both races, upon reading of the colonization movement will say they wish it had succeeded. Others will affirm the principle of separatism was not then, and is not now, a solution. David Walker, the Negro propagandist, expressed it for many when he wrote in 1829, "Tell us no more about colonization, for America is as much our country as it is yours."[25]

Slave life was immensely varied.[26] It ranged from the degraded and bestial to a degree of respect and honor. In some ways, the quality of life depended upon the individual slave, just as it does among free men. In a much greater measure, however, the nature of the institution, and the character of one's master determined the nature of the slave's life.

Slaves were conscious of class distinction according to the amount which might have been paid for one, and the nature of work to which he was assigned. A slave for whom a man had paid $1,000 would commonly "lord it over" one purchased for $700. House servants were considered privileged in comparison with field hands, and slaves of lighter color were often held in higher esteem than those who were darker. This latter distinction was evidently due to the obvious presence of "white blood" in the lighter Negroes.

The labor of the field hands was at best difficult and tiresome. The long rows which must be cultivated or picked, the monotonous routine, and the lack of incentive all con-

---

[25]*Appeal to the Colored Citizens of the World*, in Barbour, *op. cit.*, p. 25. For the complete document see David Walker, *Walker's Appeal in Four Articles*, which is combined in one cover with Henry Highland Garnet's *An Address to the Slaves of the United States of America*, edited by William Lorenz Katz (New York: Arno Press, 1969).

[26]One of the more sympathetic accounts of slave life is found in J. Winston Coleman, Jr., *Slavery Times in Kentucky* (Chapel Hill, 1940). An exceedingly valuable original source is Frederick Law Olmsted, *The Slave States* (Reprinted, New York, 1959). See also *Unwritten History of Slavery*, ed. by Social Science Institute, Fisk University, Washington: microcard edition, 1968).

tributed toward a life which was hardly enviable. Slaves who achieved some skill, such as wood working, were at times accorded privileges not granted field hands. It was common for them to be hired out to neighboring plantations as need arose. In such instances the master received, of course, the major portion of the compensation which the other plantation paid.

The lot of slaves who had kind masters was very different from that where masters were cruel. Some masters believed that while they owned the *labor* of their servants, they did not own their *persons*. Such slaves were protected by a certain ethic from cruel or inhuman treatment. But the master who conceived himself as owning not only the labor, but the persons of his slaves, might not accept any form of ethical restraint in their treatment. Corporal punishment could be meted out with complete impunity by this kind of master, and the bodies of the slave women might also be considered his property.

Life was especially difficult for slaves who had cruel overseers, or overseers who functioned for absentee masters. A significant number of plantations were owned by wealthy people who lived in the North. These owners expected a profit from their investment, and sought to guarantee this by paying their overseers according to the measure of profit which was made each year.

The effect of this arrangement was to encourage harshness on the part of overseers, while the owners, being absent, were deprived of that measure of understanding which was more commonly the lot of owners who lived on their plantations. Those who have always been free may find it difficult to appreciate what it was like to have one's fate so completely determined by factors beyond his control.

Food, clothing, and housing, as well as a modicum of medical care, were commonly provided by the master, although these benefits were very limited. Food consisted largely of corn and fat meat (supplemented by items which the slave might obtain secretly). Most slave clothing con-

sisted of "linsey-woolsey," a very uncomfortable fabric by
modern standards. Women wore a sort of shift, while men
wore breeches and shirts. Children would wear shirts in
winter, and often nothing in summer.

Slave cabins were usually of rough hewn timbers, perhaps twelve by fifteen feet, one room, with a dirt floor.
Cooking was done over the open hearth. Sanitary facilities
were rudimentary or often totally lacking. Water supply
would ordinarily come from a common well. Glass windows were seldom found in slave cabins. If there were
windows they were sometimes covered by oiled paper in
winter, and left open in summer.

The extent to which the problems of the modern Negro
family are attributable to the slavery system is a subject of
much debate. Suffice it to say here, slavery placed the family institution under almost insuperable difficulties, the results of which are doubtless profound.

In the first place, the marriage of slaves did not have the
legal standing which was accorded whites. Especially where
masters conceived themselves as having property in the persons — not simply the labor — of their slaves would it be difficult for a slave couple to "belong" to each other as husband
and wife. The ceremony of "marriage" among slaves often
simply involved the act of "jumping over the broom stick."
This was hardly a means of impressing upon a man and
woman the sanctity of their relationship.

Whether a husband and wife, or parents and children,
might be sold away from each other was largely a matter
decided by the character of the master. The law placed no
more restriction upon his disposition of slaves than upon sale
of any other "property." After all, Chief Justice Taney of
the Supreme Court was to declare in the Dred Scott Decision of 1857 that there was no legal difference between
"property in a slave and other property." Ironically, Taney
declared that "the rights of property are united with the
rights of person, and placed on the same ground by the
fifth amendment to the Constitution, which provides that no

person shall be deprived of life, liberty, and property, without due process of law."

But had not the slave been deprived of his liberty? Perhaps, but he was not a "person" in the legal sense. "The unhappy black race," Taney wrote, "were separated from the white by indelible marks, and laws long before established, and were never thought of or spoken of except as property. . . ." Therefore, the master's right of property transcended the slave's right to his person, and when the Constitution began with the words, "We the people," it obviously did not include slaves.

Presumably, Christian masters would never separate slave families by sale, for they were obliged to see them not simply as "legal property," but as persons of worth for whom Christ died. At times this subjected such masters to greater burdens, as when they came to have more slaves than their plantations could support, but they were unable to emancipate them due to restrictive laws.

Masters who had no inclination to respect the persons of their slaves sold them from their families with little hesitation. One of the factors which brought James A. Garfield into the lists against slavery was Corydon Fuller's account of the sale of some children from their mother. This became increasingly common as plantations in the upper South suffered from soil exhaustion and oversupply of slaves.

The impact of such a system upon the roles of slave parents is not difficult to imagine. Insecurity and irresponsibility were characteristic. Marital fidelity was expected of those slaves who were Christian, but even here the system served as a major hindrance to family stability.[27] Church records are replete with efforts to discipline slave members in matters of social and sexual morality. A classic example of this problem was faced by the church in South Elkhorn, Kentucky. A minute dated 4th Sat. June, 1816, says:

----

[27]Coleman, *op. cit.*, p. 57 f. For a contemporary dimension of this problem see Silberman, *op. cit.*, p. 226 f.

> Joanna Brother Pollards Woman, Came forward
> and informed the Church that She had taken a Man
> for a Husband who had two other professed Wives
> living, one of them in Virginia the other fifty Miles
> from him. She therefore wanted Counsel on her
> Case. It appeared that the above mentioned man was
> and is debarred from Visiting his former Wives it
> is the opinion of the Church that Joanna is at liberty
> to continue with him as Husband and Wife.[28]

This action was taken by the congregation immediately after having excommunicated for adultery two women, one white, the other slave. The ethical ambivalence of the situation is evident. Yet, the church members who granted Joanna the "liberty" to live with a man who had been separated by the "system" from his two former wives apparently saw no other alternative "under the circumstances."

The tendency of the slave system was to encourage a matriarchal structure of the family. Even though the husband might not be sold away from the wife, the limitations placed upon their relationship required the mother to assume the major role in the child's upbringing. This matriarchal tendency is yet found among many American Negro families, although it is uncertain whether it is altogether traceable to slavery. It may be the result of more immediate circumstances.[29]

Laws prohibiting the education of slaves were particularly offensive to many Christians. As has been noted, these laws were passed in reaction to the slave revolts — uprisings which were attributed to their reading "incendiary" literature. At one time delivery of these materials through the mails had been blocked by southern postmasters. When the courts forbade this, the option of depriving slaves of the ability to read was chosen.[30]

---

[28]South Elkhorn Minutes, June, 1816 (Library, Lexington Theological Seminary).

[29]For a contemporary survey of this problem see Ernest W. Burgess and Harvey J. Locke, *The Family*, (New York, 1963), p. 77 f.

[30]Jesse Macy, *Anti-Slavery Crusade* (New Haven, 1919), pp. 75, 76.

To enable slaves to become educated was inconsistent with their bondage. Of course, many masters would have educated and liberated them. This was not, however, the opinion of the majority in positions of political influence. In a sense, such laws were realistic if slavery were to be preserved, for as Alexander Campbell said, "Knowledge and slavery are incompatible."[31]

To Campbell, such laws were fundamentally immoral. "Any law or statute," he said, "that prevents man from acting morally or religiously . . . is not only opposed to the genius of our government and constitution, but is, in its very nature, tyrannical, unjust, and impious. . . ."[32] He viewed such laws as being in distinct contradiction to the Biblical command that masters render to their servants "that which is just and equal." "Is it *just* and *equal*," he asked, that a slave should receive "no more education than his mule?"

Thomas Campbell, father of Alexander, had once opened a school in Burlington, Kentucky, only to leave that state when his instruction of some slaves one Sunday brought a warning from citizens of the town. The older reformer resolved never again to live where he could be intimidated for teaching the Bible or the rudiments of education to the ignorant.[33]

These acts prohibiting education of slaves were especially burdensome to the Christian master who took seriously the spiritual welfare of his household. How could one instruct his slaves in spiritual matters while forbidding them the education essential to moral decision? Alexander Campbell declared that the master could not be emancipated from moral responsibility to his slaves by laws prohibiting their public

---

[31]*Millennial Harbinger*, Alexander Campbell; W. K. Pendleton, editors (Bethany, Virginia, 1830-1870), (1830), p. 47.

[32]*Ibid.*, (1830), p. 132.

[33]Robert Richardson, *Memoirs of Alexander Campbell* (2 vols., Cincinnati, 1897), I, p. 494 f.

education. He should open a "school in his own house or on his own premises" where he could fulfill this obligation to them. If he could not do this, the master ought to free himself of the responsibility by manumitting the slaves. This was a major reason Campbell had emancipated the slaves which had come to him on the occasion of his marriage.[34]

Not all slaves with inquisitive minds were so fortunate. Some were forced to learn through less favorable means, as did Frederick Douglass.[35] Others never had opportunity to learn at all. While the personal tragedy of such deprivation may be difficult to comprehend, it has not yet disappeared from the American scene.

It is remarkable that despite such disadvantages the slaves should have made the rich contribution to American culture which is represented in the spiritual and in their folk lore. These songs and stories were richly symbolic, and many of them expressed profound insight. Especially significant seem to have been the many triumphs of Br'er Rabbit, who is interpreted as representing the victory of the weak over the strong.[36]

The fellowship of the church provided one of the few stimulating opportunities for the slave. He might, indeed, receive some sort of vicarious pleasure through watching the "goings on" at the "big house" of a master when neighbors came to a party. But on religious occasions he could be more of a participant. There he might meet fellows from neighboring plantations and participate in the activities of worship. In services of Negro congregations the slaves would naturally be less inhibited than in those services shared with masters. However, the growing fear which followed the revolts of Vesey and Nat Turner caused

---

[34]*Millennial Harbinger*, (1849), p. 249; See also Coleman, "The Darker Side," in *Slavery Times in Kentucky*, p. 245 f.

[35]*Life and Times of Frederick Douglass* (Hartford, Conn., 1881), pp. 45 f., 105. This is a classic autobiography of a former slave.

[36]Bernard Wolfe, "Uncle Remus and the Malevolent Rabbit," *Commentary*, July, 1949, pp. 31-44.

many masters to look with disfavor upon any large slave gatherings in which white men were not present.

The lot of the slave was at worst cruel and inhuman. At best it was restrictive, and frustrated fulfillment of one's personality. (Even from this distance it seems ironical to speak of slaves as having "personalities.") Slaves who were ill treated often spent every waking hour seeking ways of escape. But even where masters were kind, many slaves yet sought freedom. There were those who "found their place" within the system, and enjoyed the security discovered in their master's favor. But kind treatment did not assure obedient and gentle slaves. Some of the most rebellious were to be found on plantations where masters were gentle. This seeming paradox was explained by John Fee when he said, "Hog and hominy are no compensation for lost manhood."[37]

The Slaves of Slaves

When one views the slave system from the standpoint of the master he may see a form of bondage different in nature, but in many ways equally detrimental to the master's humanity and dignity. When the southern states began to pass the laws forbidding slave education, Campbell exclaimed, "What a stupendous monument of the slavery of the whites to the blacks!"[38]

This was no simple, poetic expression. Campbell was an astute observer and analyst. To masters he once wrote, "You may be more really slaves than those you designate by that name." Were not many masters more afraid of their slaves than their slaves were of them? Did they not garrison their houses by night, and dwell in fear of insurrection? For this reason, he was as interested in the "emancipation of masters" from the bondage of fear, as the emancipation of slaves from the bondage of forced labor.[39]

---

[37]Sinfulness of Slaveholding (New York, 1851), p. 21.
[38]*Millennial Harbinger*, (1830), p. 131.
[39]*Ibid.*, (1830), pp. 128, 129.

But masters were bound by other cords than those of fear. Mastery imposed subtle, but very real, restrictions upon one's freedom. In the "big house" there was little privacy. The constant presence of slaves who were regarded as semimembers of the family was a mixed blessing, to say the least. The ambivalence of the situation occasioned no small amount of tension. The house slave was so near, and yet so far. He could share in the affection of the family, could be secure within its circle, and was privy to most of its secrets. BUT, he was still a slave — an item of property. That fact could never be forgotten even amidst the most favorable circumstances. The result was that many slaves developed an inscrutability which hid their true thoughts behind a mask of servility.[40]

Just as there were different kinds of masters, there were different kinds of slaves. It is remarkable that so many of them were well disposed toward their owners, so intensely loyal to their families. The nature and tendency of slavery was to produce the opposite attitudes of frustration, irritability, and impatience. The house servant might repress such feelings lest he be sent into the fields, but there were subtle as well as overt ways of making the master's life miserable.

The church occasionally became involved in such problems as it sought to exercise discipline over its members. The congregation at Mayslick, Kentucky, once appointed a committee to investigate a charge that a certain "Sister Johnson" was mistreating a servant. The committee composed of men "waited on Sister Johnson, and heard her case, which was her unjustafyable treatment towards her black girl — by whiping her severly." The committee interviewed Sister Johnson and concluded that she "done no more than one of us would have done." Whether the committee heard the slave's side of the story we are not told.[41]

---

[40]Douglass, *op. cit.*, p. 98.

[41]Minute Book, Mayslick Christian Church, Mason County, Kentucky, January 9, 1850 (Library, Lexington Theological Seminary).

The minutes of the congregation at Pleasant Grove, Kentucky, reveal a similar problem. There a committee was charged to investigate an incident which had been brought to the attention of the church. In this instance both parties were members of the congregation. "Margarett a Sister of colour of br. Scoggans" was charged with "dispitifully attempting to scald her Mistress," Mrs. Scoggans. The committee continued the investigation for two months, when, for some unknown reason, the matter was dropped.

Viewing such situations, the clerk of Pleasant Grove confided to the minutes, "O that the church could be freed from sutch perplexing difficulties."[42]

It is obvious that the family of a master could not be insulated from the demoralizing tendencies of slavery. An astute analysis of this is to be found in Campbell's "Tract for the People of Kentucky." This "Tract" was occasioned by the Constitutional Convention which was to be held in Kentucky in 1849. Campbell, whose religious reformation had had great influence in that state, felt strongly that the propitious time had come in which the citizens of the commonwealth could rid themselves of the blight of the system. The "Tract" was issued about the time of Henry Clay's famous "Lexington Letter," and became associated with it in the minds of Kentuckians.

Campbell's analysis "pulled no punches." First, he noted the inconsistency of committing children to the care of slaves, while forbidding to those slaves the benefits of education.

> What shall we think of the Christian wisdom, piety and paternal affection of those Christian parents, who, reckless of the associations and intimacies of their own dear offspring, commit them, from the nursery, to the inmates of negro kitchens and negro

---

[42]Pleasant Grove Minutes, November, 1845; December, 1845 (Library, Lexington Theological Seminary).

cabins generally more degraded in morals and im-
piety than in condition and circumstance?[43]

Campbell realized that there were parents who sought
to counter "these sinister influences," but their efforts were
"occasional and sporadic, while the opposing and contami-
nating influence" was constant.

The psychological impact of slavery upon the households
of masters was likewise a source of concern. Campbell recognized that cruel masters were less common than kind, but
"the tendency of the relation" was "to degrade rather than
to elevate the servant, to render haughty and tyrannical the
master." This tendency was "unfavorable to the proper
moral education and development of children." The harsh
way in which commandments were often given to slaves was
naturally imitated by the master's children, even when they
played with slave children. The habits thus formed were
greatly detrimental to the development of character in ac-
cordance with Christian principles.[44]

The burden of supervising slave labor was of no small
consequence. By nature slavery undermined initiative. The
slave had little motivation to excel, except as this might in
some way be attached to privilege. For the most part meth-
ods of work were slow. In times of urgency, therefore, the
whip of the overseer was considered by some masters to be a
"necessary evil." Needless to say, some masters made common use of such "urgent measures."

Even so, slaves developed many ways of exercising certain "freedoms" within the system. Stealing, "triflin," or
loafing when the master's back was turned, became highly
developed arts. While these would frustrate the overseer or

---

[43]*Millennial Harbinger*, (1849), p. 250. Even such an apologist
for slavery as William Harper admitted the degenerating effect of
slavery upon the character of the masters' families. *Pro-Slavery
Argument, as Maintained by the Most Distinguished Writers of the
Southern States* (Charleston, 1852), p. 61 f.

[44]*Millennial Harbinger* (1849), p. 251. See also W. J. Cash, *The
Mind of the South* (New York, 1956), p. 98.

master, even corporal punishment reached a point of diminishing returns. For the sake of sanity one had to learn to live within the pace set by the system.[45]

Meanwhile, the economic inefficiency of slavery bore heavily upon the master, especially upon the conscientious master. When a master made an investment in a slave he immediately became concerned for the slave's presence, his health, and his efficiency. A fugitive meant economic loss to the master. So did the sickness of a slave. Therefore, masters were obliged to care for their slaves, if not for humane reasons, for reasons economic and practical.

More than once did the mistress of a household go into the slave quarters, as did the wife of John C. Calhoun, to minister to slaves who were ill of the "pox." As somewhat self-sustaining economic units, plantations were forced to provide medical aid of sorts, and this usually fell to the mistress.

Meanwhile, the master was obliged to provide for the needs of the slave child until such time as he could begin to work, and to care for the aged Negro after his working days were over.

Having a significant investment in the slave's labor, the master would commonly protect him from work which was known to be too difficult. In the deep South, where cultivation of some crops required the heavy labor of "ditching," it was common to hire roving gangs of Irish laborers. These could be paid modest wages, and if one was overcome by heat, or fell as result of an accident, the master had no further responsibility. Loading cotton was likewise often done by free labor. One did not want a thousand-dollar investment on the receiving end of a bale of cotton as it slid down the plank onto a riverboat. It was better to pay a wage and not be held responsible. As one master explained to Frederick Law Olmsted, who was visiting him, "If a Negro dies, it's a considerable loss, you know."[46]

---

[45]Olmsted, *op. cit.*, p. 76.
[46]*Ibid.*, p. 76.

The economic responsibilities of the master, as compared with those of the northern industrialist, was the theme of a famous book by a southern apologist, George Fitzhugh.[47] In *Cannibals All,* Fitzhugh contrasted the two forms of labor, noting how the northern industrialist would hire laborers, work them until their health was broken, and then cast them aside. By comparison, Fitzhugh considered slave labor humane. The master had an investment in the welfare of his slave, and was responsible for his care as long as he lived. Of course, labor abuses in the North did not make the lot of the slave any better. He was probably completely unaware of such matters.

Even more burdensome, however, was the ethical responsibility which rested upon the kind master. Many of them sought to realize in their time the patriarchal ideal which they saw in the Old Testament days of Abraham. The patriarchs had "servants" who were members of their households, and the relationship seems not to have been fraught with undue difficulties. But American slavery was hardly like that of the patriarchs, as many Christian masters discovered in the course of time. Nothing the Bible may have said about slavery could justify the American system.

Kind masters often felt themselves trapped within the system. Certain facts confronted them: They had slaves, whether by past purchase, or, as was often the case, by inheritance; they were responsible for them, even though their labor might be inefficient, the plantation might not support their numbers, or the master tire of the constant stress of supervising their work and other activities. Masters were limited in what they could do to be free.

Sale of slaves which involved family separation was not a "live option" to many slaveowners, for it did violence to Christian and humane principles. Yet, emancipation was itself restricted by state laws. A master who freed a slave was commonly required to guarantee the good conduct and wel-

---

[47]*Cannibals All! or, Slaves Without Masters* (1851).

fare of the freedman, or to see that he left the state. These laws were rooted in the white fear of the effect which free Negroes had upon slave population — a fear abundantly reinforced by David Walker's, *Appeal to the Colored Citizens of the World.*

It may be seen, therefore, that the master who wished to be relieved of the burden of the system was seriously limited in his options. The bonds which bound the slave also bound him. It was to factors such as this that Campbell referred when he said, "The emancipation of masters is full as much an object near to my heart as the emancipation of slaves."[48]

There are numerous instances of masters who went to great lengths to be relieved of their burden. It appears that Barton Stone removed from Kentucky to Illinois in order to disqualify himself from a bequest which made him responsible for slaves which had been willed to his children.[49]

Dr. James T. Barclay, owner of Monticello, was almost kept from fulfilling a mission to the Near East because he possessed slaves. Barclay had inherited a family of slaves who lived on the plantation. Upon being called to represent the American Christian Missionary Society, he offered the slaves their freedom. Since he could not be responsible for them in keeping with the law, it would be necessary for them to leave Virginia. This they did not want to do. Barclay therefore "sold" three of them for a "nominal" figure to a fellow member of the church in Charlottesville who was known as a good master. This man would not, however, assume responsibility for the fourth, an elderly woman. Confronted by this impasse, Barclay provided for her a cabin of her choice on the plantation, established a trust fund for her support, and went on his mission. However, the fact that he was still technically a slave owner subjected him to vi-

---

[48]*Millennial Harbinger*, (1849), p. 249.
[49]Barton W. Stone, *Biography of Elder Barton W. Stone Written by Himself: With Additions and Reflections by Elder John Rogers* (Cincinnati, 1847), p. 293.

cious criticism among members of the church in the North. To them it was unthinkable that a "manstealer" should be a missionary. Yet, the only ways Barclay could have been "emancipated" from this slave would have been to force her to leave Virginia, or to refuse the assignment in the Near East and remain in Virginia where he could be responsible for her use of freedom.[50]

Numeris Humber represents an even more pathetic example of a master who sought "emancipation." Humber migrated to Kansas with the deliberate intention of setting free his slaves and settling them there upon land which he would give them. When he sought to make the necessary legal arrangements, however, he found to his dismay that it would not be possible for free Negroes to hold land in Kansas.

Humber was therefore confronted with the choice of emancipating his slaves even though they had little prospect of an adequate livelihood, or remaining their master in order that they might have a larger measure of security. He chose to keep them for their sakes, even though he had sought so earnestly to be free from the bonds of mastery.[51]

From this it may be seen that if the slaves were slaves of masters, there was a very real sense in which masters were slaves of slaves. Slavery was a system of *mutual* bondage. When "a Southern Clergyman" (Iveson L. Brookes of South Carolina) protested Campbell's "Tract" and Clay's "Lexington Letter," he said:

> Why will deranged fanatics and selfish demagogues intermeddle with this divine Institution and resort to every subterfuge of lies and the use of basest misrepresentations to subvert slavery and ruin the master and the slave!

---

[50]*North-Western Christian Magazine*, edited by John Boggs, (Cincinnati, 1854-1858), I (1854), p. 254 f.

[51]Rosetta B. Hastings, *Personal Recollections of Pardee Butler*, (Cincinnati, 1889), p. 65 f.

Brookes felt that neither Clay nor Campbell had the right to "meddle" with this "divine institution," or to "destroy the vested rights of slave holders. . . ."[52]

Little did the "southern Clergyman" seem to realize that it was by those same "vested rights" that masters themselves became slaves of slaves.

---

[52]A Southern Clergyman [Iveson L. Brookes], *A Defence of Southern Slavery, Against the Attacks of Henry Clay and A. Campbell* (Hamburg, S. C., 1851), ii. Copy in New York Public Library.

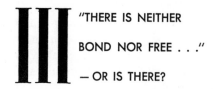

III "THERE IS NEITHER BOND NOR FREE . . ."
— OR IS THERE?

The system of "mutual bondage" which we have just described was created through the confluence of two vastly different streams which entered the new world at the beginning of the nineteenth century. The one was a movement toward freedom, composed largely of white men. The other was a movement into bondage, composed of black men. The difference between these two streams, so alien to each other, can hardly be overemphasized.

The one stream found its source in human aspiration toward liberty, both political and religious. The other flowed from the bitter springs of prejudice and avarice. The first stream has been commonly recognized as a clear source of our contemporary way of life. The second has been largely ignored, although our ancestors drank deeply of its bitter waters.

It is necessary to our study that each of these be examined if we are to understand the meaning of their flowing together. As we do so, it may well appear that here were two very different worlds. In a sense they were. The African suffocating between the decks of a slave ship *was* in a very different world, socially, intellectually, and spiritually, from that of the white immigrant whose circumstances might be little better, but who saw before him a life of enlarged liberty.

Yet, in a more fundamental sense, they were in the same world — God's world. It was His will that freemen and bondmen should meet in one society — the church — and that the fellowship discovered there would transform their social relationship. What happened in that meeting is the subject of this chapter.

The body variously known congregationally as "Christian Churches" or "Churches of Christ," was the result of several efforts toward reformation which developed in the early nineteenth century. They were drawn together in the course of time because they shared the same convictions:

First, they were appalled by the way in which sectarianism frustrated the mission of the church.

Second, they sought recovery of the unity of the church in order that it might better fulfill its mission.

Third, they believed that unity could be realized through recovery of the faith, fellowship, and life of the early Christian community.[1]

These men shared the long tradition of the "restorationists" or "restitutionists," but they did so with the catholic intention of recovering the unity of the church. In this they were unique.

Movements embodying these ideals with various nuances developed in New England, Virginia and the Carolinas, Kentucky, and Pennsylvania. In New England, Elias Smith and Abner Jones led their congregations to espouse the Bible alone as their rule of faith and practice, and to take the name "Christian" as their sole designation.

In Virginia, James O'Kelly led a similar movement within Methodism. He and his associates opposed the introduction of episcopacy in the Baltimore Conference of 1784, and subsequently withdrew to form the "Republican Methodist

---

[1]For a discussion of these developments see Dean E. Walker, *Adventuring for Christian Unity* (Birmingham, England: Berean Press, 1935), Winfred E. Garrison and Alfred T. DeGroot, *The Disciples of Christ, a History* (St. Louis, 1948); James DeForest Murch, *Christians Only* (Cincinnati: Standard Publishing, 1962).

Church."[2] When O'Kelly met the reformer, Rice Haggard, under his influence they were to assume the name, "Christian."

While opposed to each other concerning the issue of church polity, Asbury and O'Kelly were united in their opposition to slavery. Asbury records in his *Journal* their confrontation with proslavery members in the Conference of 1785, saying:

> Brother O'Kelly let fly at them, and they were made angry enough; we, however, came off with whole bones, and our business in conference was finished in peace.[3]

In Kentucky, where the Great Revival had brought men of various denominations together, Barton Stone and others led in a unitive movement, similarly called by the simple name, "Christian." These men once formed themselves into a separate presbytery, but upon coming to believe that this was divisive, they wrote *The Last Will and Testament of the Springfield Presbytery,* and it was dissolved.[4]

In Pennsylvania, a "Christian Association" was formed for the promotion of Christian unity by a group living in the environs of Washington. They were led by Thomas Campbell, a recent immigrant from Ireland and minister of the Seceder Anti-Burgher Presbyterian Church. The Association published a manifesto entitled, *Declaration and Address of the Christian Association of Washington* (1809). This document affirmed that "the church of Christ on earth

---

[2]W. E. MacClenny, *The Life of Rev. James O'Kelly* (Reprinted, Indianapolis, n.d.) pp. 81-120; Thomas B. Neely, *A History of the Origin and Development of the Governing Conference in Methodism* (Cincinnati, 1892), p. 163.

[3]Francis Asbury, *Journal and Letters,* ed. by Elmer T. Clark and others (3 vols., Nashville, 1958), I, p. 488.

[4]*Last Will and Testament of the Springfield Presbytery* (Reprinted, Indianapolis: International Convention of Disciples of Christ, 1949); William G. West, *Barton Warren Stone* (Nashville, 1954), p. 19 f.

ᵢₛ one," and set forth the principles through which they believed that unity could be realized.[5]

These people, sometimes simply called, "Disciples," were protestant in their acceptance of the authority of Scripture. But they were also catholic in their concern for unity. Their movement originated in a period when the spirit of freedom was spread throughout the land. It rapidly expanded along the frontier, and came to have its greatest strength on the border of North and South. It was, therefore, inevitably involved in the slavery controversy.

This plea for "Christian unity" was addressed to the "Christians in all the sects." Its motive was missionary. The plan seemed simple, and the principles valid. They were obviously not speaking to slaves when they issued their *Declaration,* but to Christians caught in another form of bondage — bondage to human creeds and sectarian loyalties.

Yet, if the principles of the manifesto were valid for the breaking down of the sectarian walls which divided men, ought they not also be effective in bridging the vast chasm which stood between freeman and slave? *If the "church of Christ on earth is one," must its unity not break through all forms of human distinction?*

The story of how these men found a new sense of unity in Christ has often been told. But what happened when the two cultural streams of freedom and bondage flowed into the church? How "one" did master and slave, white and black become? It is our present task to study this neglected story.

While several religious bodies deliberately cultivated Negro congregations in the South,[6] the "Christians" or "Dis-

---

[5]*Declaration and Address of the Christian Association of Washington* (Reprinted, Indianapolis: International Convention of Disciples of Christ, 1949); Robert Richardson, *Memoirs of Alexander Campbell* (2 vols., Cincinnati, 1897), I, p. 494 f.

[6]See Carter G. Woodson, *History of the Negro Church* (Washington, 1921), pp. 100-166. A more recent and very succinct work is E. Franklin Frazier, *The Negro Church in America* (New York: Schocken Books, 1964).

ciples" encouraged the membership of both masters and slaves in the same church. Prior to 1860 there were only four Negro Christian congregations in Kentucky.[7] It is possible that desire to supervise the religious life of the slaves, or unwillingness to support separate congregations for them, may have been factors in this early pattern of common membership. The sources, however, support the impression that these reformers felt such social or racial separation was inconsistent that their plea for Christian unity.

But if the ideal called for unity, the real made it difficult to attain. It did not seem possible to obliterate completely the cultural gap which existed between master and slave. Even where there was the desire it was difficult to erase the social distinctions which characterized their relationship.

Nonetheless, it was steadfastly maintained that all were "one in Christ," and it is evident that at least in some congregations there existed a rich fellowship between masters and servants which was fondly remembered in after years. Writing in retrospect of those associations in the church at Nashville, Tolbert Fanning said, "they prayed, sang, exhorted and broke bread together, as members of one family."[8]

Slave Membership

Slaves were admitted into church membership on the same *Biblical* conditions as were masters: confession of faith and baptism. The following account from the Minutes of the Walnut Spring Church, near Strasburg, Virginia, is typical:

---

[7]Claude Walker, "Negro Disciples in Kentucky, 1840-1925," Typescript B. D. Thesis. (Lexington, Kentucky: College of the Bible, 1959), pp. 5-8.

[8]*The Religious Historian,* edited by Tolbert Fanning (Nashville, 1872-) I (1872), pp. 89, 90.

March 23, 1822

At a Church meeting held in Strasburg Derostes
F. Ladley — and Esther Beard were received into
Fellowship. Also Jordan a slave belonging to Van-
meter as to his experience; and admited to baptism,
and into Fellowship as a Church Member as far as
the Nature of his case, and the Laws of the Country
will admit.

D. Stickley Clerk Protem   Peter Boyer Mod.[9]

From the Biblical standpoint, the baptism of Jordan in-
ducted him into the unhindered fellowship of Christ. But
socially speaking, this was limited by "the nature of his case,
and the Laws of the Country." In such simple language did
the clerk describe the profound issue which the church in
every generation must face. This issue may be stated in the
form of a question: *Is the church's nature to be determined
by the social order in which it finds itself, or by the Cross of
Christ?*

A free Negro named Rachel Hunter was admitted into
the fellowship of Walnut Spring and "acknowledged as a
member of the Church of Christ" on June 4, 1825.

The old roll of the Walnut Spring congregation included a
number of Negroes, whose names were interspersed among
those of their white masters.

Rachel Hunter	(Black woman)	Removed
Elizabeth	(Do)	Removed
Thomas Cotterill	(Elder)	Disowned
Jacob	(a slave)	Removed

----

[9]Minute Book of the Christian Church in Strasburg at the Walnut
Spring school house. Unpublished, unpaged. Carolina Discipliana
Library, Wilson, N.C. Throughout this chapter it would seem cum-
bersome always to indicate through the usual form errors in spelling
or punctuation in material quoted. Special care has been exercised to
reproduce the entries accurately, hence the usual form will not be
used.

Sarah Spencer	(colored	)	

Benjamin Jonny	(colored	)	
Richard	(Ditto	)	Sold
Frank	(Do	)	"

Martin Jones	(Color'd	)	Removed

All these were Negroes save Thomas Cotterill, whose eldership was designated in the same column as the Negroes' slavehood. The Church at Walnut Spring continued to receive Negro members as late as 1866.

The "Church of Christ at Concord," Pantego, North Carolina, had thirty-six charter members, two of whom were slaves — Gideon and Christmas. These were soon joined by others, among whom were Mingo and Nancy. In July, 1840, Sally was one of thirteen persons baptized into the Church. Moses, Jerry and Calloway were received in September of 1843.[10]

By the close of the year 1844, the Concord Church numbered one hundred forty-nine members, of whom twenty-eight were slaves. Among these were Luke, Wilson, Mingo, William, George, Christmas, Eda, Letitia, Susan, Keziah, Sylva, Nancy, Eda (of Lanier), and Matilda Ann.

Slaves often transferred their membership from one congregation to another. Thus it was "on motion agreed," by the Concord Church, "that Sister Celia (a Slave) a member from the Pungo River Church be received as a member of this church and her name enrolled on our list of members." Whether such transfers of membership were because of the removal of masters, or the sale of slaves, is not often indicated.

In Kentucky, the pattern was similar, although the church records in that state seldom used the term "slave." These

---

[10]Minutes of the Church of Christ at Concord, Pantego, North Carolina. Unpublished, unpaged. Carolina Discipliana Library, Wilson, N.C. Hereafter designated Pantego Minutes.

members were usually designated as "belonging to" some-
one, or as "Bro. _____'s man," or "Mr. _____'s woman."
Whether this was simple conformity to common usage, or
deliberate euphemism is not clear.

Cane Ridge, the mother of a number of Kentucky congregations, had a large body of colored members. The roll
of June 15, 1838, listed the names of the "Coloured Members of the Church at Cane-Ridge," of which there were
seventy-two of a total of two hundred and twenty-two. By
1852 the white members numbered one hundred and twenty-
four, and the colored members seventy-one, some of whom
were marked as deceased, or removed. Among the latter was
George Rogers, who was perhaps a fugitive, for it is said
that he had "gone to Canada West."[11]

What proportion of the colored members of the Cane
Ridge Church remained slave is not clear. The biographer
of David Purviance, who was closely associated with the
congregation, says, "A majority of the members of the Cane-
ridge Church, that owned slaves, liberated them; believing
it to be right to do unto the poor unfortunate colored people,
as they would wish others to do to them, in like circumstances."[12] Barton Stone also spoke of the tide of emancipation which followed the Great Revival on the frontier. It
seemed to him perfectly natural that the Gospel should bear
such social fruits.

It is noteworthy that the Lawrence Creek Christian
Church in Mason County, Kentucky, originated in the movement among the Baptists known as "Friends of Humanity."[13] In 1805 a number of Baptist ministers and churches
were expelled from the Bracken, Elkhorn, and North Dis-

---

[11]Church Book, Christian Church at Cane Ridge. Unpublished,
unpaged. Library, Lexington Theological Seminary.

[12]Purviance, *op. cit.,* p. 48.

[13]For discussions of this interesting movement see Asa E. Martin,
*The Anti-Slavery Movement in Kentucky, Prior to 1850. Filson Club
Publications, XXIX* (Louisville, 1918), p. 39 f.; Coleman, *op. cit.,*
p. 293 f. Martin notes that the "Friends of Humanity" were allowed
to keep slaves too old or too young to care for themselves.

trict Associations because of their advocacy of emancipation. Called "Friends to Humanity" or "Emancipators," they organized themselves into the "Baptized Licking-Locust Association, Friends to Humanity." There were eleven ministers and thirteen laymen in this original group.[14] In 1808, these "emancipating Baptists" formed the Kentucky Abolition Society, "the first distinctly antislavery organization in the state."

There were but nine original members of this congregation, and evidently no slaves among them. This would, indeed, be expected in the instance of a group withdrawing from established Baptist congregations because of opposition to slavery.

But the pressure of maintaining an antislavery fellowship amidst the growing spirit of sectional rivalry was evidently tremendous. The clarity of the fathers' vision is not always transmitted to their children. Thus it appears that the "Friends of Humanity" principle was later abandoned by the Lawrence Creek congregation. A subsequent roll showed nine colored members of a total of ninety-five, while the roll of 1840 gave "a list of Colloured Brothers and Sisters" among whom were:

> Mr. E. Berry's Betty
> "   R. Downing Jerry & wife
> Mr. P. Gordons Aima.[15]

It is not clear when the Lawrence Creek Church first admitted slaveholders to fellowship, but by 1840 the practice

---

[14]The "Emancipators" at Lawrence Creek recorded their constitution as a church saying, "The Brethren of Lawrence Creek Known by the name of the Friends of humanity after Frequently Calling on the Lord for direction In duty and after due Conference amongst Ourselves We have Constituted in a Church — March 22, 1807." Church Register and Record, Lawrence Creek Christian Church, Mason County, Kentucky. Library, Lexington Theological Seminary.

[15]This was probably part of the general decline in antislavery activity. The Kentucky Abolition Society died in 1827. Coleman, *op. cit.,* p. 294.

elicited no unusual comment in the minutes. The following extracts illustrate the condition which had come to exist:

> April 19th 1840
> The Church met & after worship Peter a Brother of Collour The property of Mr. John Bennet Presented himself for membership having Been Immersed the Lords Day Previous and was Received.
> June 14th 1840
> After A sermon From Brother R. C. Ricketts Hemey A Sister of Collour Presented Her Self and was receive.

Following a protracted meeting in January, 1855, the clerk records that:

> Coulered Sisters Harriet & Betsey Taylor the property of Sister Claracy Gordon also Washington a coulered brother belonging to Robert Downing, they all presented themselves for membership and was Received by the hand of fellowship.

The Pleasant Grove Christian Church of Jefferson County, Kentucky, is notable for its large proportion of colored members. In 1821, following early Baptist practice, it "opened a door for the reception of members and Recd by experience for Baptism Thomas a black man the property of James Vance."[16]

By 1850 the church roll of Pleasant Grove consisted of seventy-nine members — forty-two white and thirty-seven colored.

While the *Biblical* conditions for slave membership were the same as those for masters, the *social* conditions were different. Churches in the South commonly required a slave to have the permission of his master before he could become a member of the church. That this practice compromised the integrity of the Gospel, and of every man's

---

[16]Clerk's Record, Pleasant Grove Christian Church. Unpublished, unpaged. Library, Lexington Theological Seminary. Hereafter designated Pleasant Grove Minutes.

right to respond to it, may have been recognized by some. Nonetheless, the churches often made this concession to the system. In so doing, they allowed the social order to determine an important dimension of the church's life.

The following extract taken from the records of the church at Walnut Spring, Virginia, is illustrative:

> October 6th 1832 Richard was rec,d into fellowship with the Christian Church at Walnut spring schoolhouse; by permission from his master. In the following words . . .
>
> Zoar Oct 6th 1832
>
> To the Christian Church at Captain Stickley's school house:
>
> Gentlemen. This is to inform you, that my man Richard, has the privilege of being attached to your Church.
>
> Very Respectfully yours
Chaney Gatewood.
>
> Oct, 7 1832. Frank was received into fellowship with the Christian Church at Walnut spring school house; by permission from his master, In the following words. —
>
> This may Certify. That Frank, the Bearer, has my permission to Join the Christian Baptist society.
>
> Bellgrove Oct 6th 1832   Isaac Hite.[17]

One problem involved in slave membership was its tenuous character. Slaves might be kept from worship at the command of their masters. For this reason they were seldom disciplined for nonattendance as were whites.[18] A larger problem is reflected in the records, where it is indicated that slave members were often sold, or "removed." When the Providence, Kentucky, Church took up the problem of its "unknown members" in September, 1841, it

---

[17]Minute Book, Walnut Spring.

[18]Church Record and Register, Providence Christian Church, Jessamine County, Kentucky. Unpublished, unpaged. Library, Lexington Theological Seminary. November, 1821; June 1822. This church was "constituted" in 1817.

found twenty-nine, most of whom were slaves. These were stricken from the list.[19]

In spite of such social disadvantages, perusal of the records show that some slaves were very active in their churches. Such, for example, were Mingo and Prince, members of the Concord Church of Pantego, North Carolina. Often their names appear in the accounts of the congregation's activities, and it is with a sense of deep loss that their deaths are recorded by the clerk.[20]

Among other churches which had both white and colored (either free or slave) members were the congregations at Boones Creek, Washington County, Tennessee;[21] Nashville, Tennessee;[22] Canton, Missouri;[23] Columbus, Mississippi;[24] Louisville, Kentucky;[25] Leavenworth, Kansas;[26] Old Liberty, Texas;[27] Smyrna Church, King and Queen County, Virginia;[28] Antioch Christian Church, Fayette County, Kentucky;[29] and Kinston, North Carolina.[30]

[19]*Ibid.*, September, 1841.

[20]Pantego Minutes, August, 1854, and March, 1865.

[21]Church Book, Boones Creek Church of Christ, Washington County, Tennessee. Unpublished, unpaged. In possession of the congregation.

[22]*Millennial Harbinger*, (1860), p. 214.

[23]Record of the Church of Christ worshipping at Canton, Lewis County, Missouri. Unpublished. Disciples of Christ Historical Society, Nashville.

[24]The Columbus congregation had Negro members as late as World War II.

[25]*Millennial Harbinger*, (1856), p. 395.

[26]S. B. Braden, "The Early History of the Disciples of Christ in Kansas (1855-1870)," (unpublished, 1933). Disciples of Christ Historical Society, Nashville.

[27]Now Van Alstyne, Texas. Garrison and DeGroot, *op. cit.*, p. 318.

[28]*The Christian Publisher*, I (1832), pp. 185, 186. (This periodical was edited and published by T. M. Henley, Charlottesville, Va., 1832-).

[29]Church Register and Records, Antioch Christian Church, Fayette County, Ky. Unpublished, unpaged. Library, Lexington Theological Seminary.

[30]Old Clerk Record, Kinston, N.C., in Charles C. Ware, *North Carolina Disciples of Christ* (St. Louis, 1927), p. 223.

Such was the common pattern of membership among the Christian churches of the antebellum South.

Slave Life in the Church

If the churches believed the admission of slaves was a mandate of the Gospel, it was difficult to accord them the same privileges in church life which were enjoyed by their masters. Bearing a message which declared God to be "no respecter of persons," to a social order which declared some men to be bond and others free, the churches could only with difficulty obey fully the mandate of the Gospel.

"The nature of his case" seriously limited the service which a slave could perform in the church. He could lead his fellow slaves as a deacon, or perhaps as an exhorter, but it would be exceptional for a slave member to serve as an elder over his white master. Church business was almost universally conducted by the "free male members."

Since it was "natural" that white folkways predominated in congregations composed of slaves and masters, it was not uncommon for slaves to seek occasions when they could worship to themselves. In later years such gatherings were frowned upon, for defenders of "the system" never knew when they might serve as cloaks for dangerous conspiracies. Even so, slaves were equal to the occasion, devising means of hiding their activities from suspicious eyes.

After emancipation freedmen were sometimes to speak fondly of the "good times" they had when they "turned the kettle down," and worshiped without the knowledge of their masters. It was believed that placing an overturned wash tub in the center of a cabin floor, or at the door, would so absorb the sound that they could shout and sing to their hearts' content without fear that whites would hear and break up their meetings.[31]

By "the nature of their case" slaves had little opportunity

---

[31]See the very interesting collection of slave reminiscences in *Unwritten History of Slavery,* ed. by Social Science Institute, Fisk University (Washington: Microcard Editions, 1968).

to participate in the act of offering. After all, they had little to give, for they had no "income" and their talents were seldom developed. Such restrictions caused John Fee to observe that they were "mere nominal members." They had no "voice in the affairs of the Church, truth, or gospel spread." Neither did they have "means to encourage or sustain the ministration of the gospel." While slaves might occasionally be permitted to preach to their fellows, seldom did they preach to masters. Fee believed the social order ought not be permitted to condition the life of the church in such a restrictive manner.

Even more perplexing than the problem of bridging the distinctions of social class were those which grew out of the conditions of slave life as they were judged by the Bible. The paradox may be stated in this fashion: *How could the moral or ethical principles of the Christian life be expected of a people whose freedom was seriously restricted, and whose social circumstances encouraged delinquency?* If spiritual discipline were difficult for the free and advantaged, what could be expected of those who were bound, and whose circumstances were commonly degrading?

Over and again, such notations as the following appear. They depict an effort to be just in treatment of both slave and free, but the problems of the slave were obviously the more conducive to moral laxity. From Pleasant Grove minutes we read:

> February, 1822
> 1st. By motion made by Bro. Vance the Church took up the subject Relative to Maria Fethenngail and finding her guilty of adultery she therefore Excludes her.
> 2nd. By motion made by Bro. Keller, the Church took up the subject relative to Chamy a black woman and finding her guilty of adultery she excludes her.

That slave discipline was a common affair in the Providence Church is seen in the following minutes:

May 2, 1819

The Church hears a report that Willis (Bro. Bars man) has been Dancing &c & lying — the charge lying being proven the Church votes he is no more of us.

June 2, 1819

The Church hears a report that Judith (Mrs. Mc-Daniels woman) has been wicked in lying & Swearing — Has been dealt with &.c. she refuses to come forward — The Church votes she is no more of us.

March 2, 1820

Easter (J. Arnetts woman) Excluded for walking disorderly.

While the churches in Kentucky commonly exercised discipline through white members, those in North Carolina appointed slave members for the task. A minute of the Concord Church reads,

On motion agreed that Brothers Eli, Jerry, and Prince (slaves), wait on Bro. Simon (slave) to ascertain from him whether the reports in circulation about his stealing are true, and report at our April meeting.[32]

Evidently the three slaves found more than they expected, for the clerk recorded the next month that "br Simon" had been "ex communicated from the fellowship of this church for conduct to [sic] base to be mentioned."[33]

This practice continued as standard procedure in the Pantego congregation. The record speaks of action taken in July, 1847, when Mingo and Luke were "appointed a committee to examine into the conduct of Sister Rhoda of Windley (all Slave)," and to report at the next meeting. In August the case was postponed, and Wilson Respess was added to the committee. On the Saturday before the first Sunday in October, the case of "Sister Rhoda" came up,

[32]Pantego Minutes, March, 1844.
[33]*Ibid.*, April, 1844.

and "after due deliberation it was ordered that she be ex-communicated for adultery."

On occasion an erring slave might be received again into the church upon demonstration of repentance. Such was the case of Sylvia, who confessed her fault to the Pantego congregation, and was "again received into the Communion of the Church."[34]

While the church attempted to govern the moral conduct of slaves, it is not clear whether Christian masters were in any way held responsible for the behavior of their slaves. When the South Elkhorn Church was informed that "Milley belonging to Widow Allen had been dancing and also parted from her husband and taken up with another man," the Church appointed "Brethren Pollard and Neal to labour with and cite her before the Church." Milley was found guilty and consequently excluded from the Church "for the sins of Adultery and dancing and Neglecting to hear the Church."[35]

Whether the church in any way disciplined Widow Allen for Milley's conduct is not indicated. But from this distance it is not difficult to see the moral dilemma of the Christian master who legally "owned" a person whose very circumstances contributed to his rejection of the values the master professed.

The South Elkhorn Minutes record one of the more shocking transgressions committed by a slave. Under date of August, 1819, the record says, "Lucy (Capt Berrys woman) charged with Fornication & murdering her own Infant. The church took up the matter & excluded her for the same." Was excommunication from the church the only punishment Lucy received for these acts? Who was involved with her? Unfortunately the minutes say no more.

Perhaps nowhere was the dilemma of the church more evident than in its efforts to sustain the values of Christian marriage among its slave members. We have already noted

---

[34]*Ibid.*, March, 1840.
[35]South Elkhorn Minutes, December, 1822; January, 1823.

some of the problems of the slave family[36] — the tenuous nature of the husband-wife relationship; the difficulty of rearing children within circumstances of bondage; the ever-present possibility of being sold away from one another; the degrading condition which was imposed upon many by their master's insistence that not only had their labor been purchased, but their bodies as well.

While the Christian master would not, presumably, engage in such abuses, he and his slave both lived within a context where it was constantly present. As long as the church consented to live at peace within such a system occasions would inevitably arise in which its ideals would be compromised. So the church at South Elkhorn excommunicated Lucey for adultery, although it had allowed Joanna, who belonged to the same master, to continue in the church because the man with whom she was living had been separated from his two former wives by the operation of the system.[37]

The Problem of Slavery in the Worship of the Church

On occasion slaves were moved to exhort their brethren. The extension of this freedom varied, however, with time and circumstance, for slaveowners remembered that Nat Turner was a preacher. Before there were many colored congregations the demand for formally educated Negro preachers was limited.

In Kentucky, a Negro named Alexander Campbell was redeemed from slavery by a congregation, and aided in the founding of the first Negro Christian Church in that state.[38] Another former slave was Samuel Lowery, who was purchased and emancipated by the Disciples in Nashville, educated by Tolbert Fanning, and moved to Canada to preach among the fugitive slaves residing there. The Amer-

---

[36]*Supra*, p. 36 f.
[37]*Supra*, p. 38.
[38]Claude Walker, *op. cit.*, pp. 5-8.

ican Christian Missionary Society supported him in this endeavor.[39]

Isaac Scott was ordained in Raleigh, North Carolina in
1852. I. N. Walter participated in the event, reporting that
Scott was "a colored brother . . . of good talents and deep
piety." Scott planned to sail for Liberia that fall, in order
to minister to the Negroes being colonized there.[40]

Andrew Marshall was one of the most famous Negro
preachers in the South. Born a slave, he so labored as to
purchase the freedom of his wife and all his children, and
finally, when over fifty years old, he purchased himself for
six hundred dollars. Marshall founded a colored Baptist
Church in Savannah, which numbered 2,795 members by
1832.[41] Alexander Campbell visited him in 1832 and
again in 1838-1839. Describing him on the latter occasion,
Campbell said:

> I am told that, though eighty-one years old, he is,
> in truth, the ablest and best preacher in Savannah.
> I had the pleasure of an interview with him; and,
> from all that I could learn from him and others, I
> conclude that he takes more care of his flock, and
> has them in better condition, than any other Baptist
> Pastor in the country. . . . He looks as though he
> might yet live forty years: a Moses in point of con-
> stitution. Take him all in all, he is an honor to the
> race to which he belongs.[42]

Overcoming similar obstacles in order to enter the ministry
was the Kentucky slave Abram Williams. Abram belonged
to an uncle of John Augustus Williams. Young Williams

---

[39]Isaac Errett, "Report of the American Christian Missionary Society, February 1, 1860," *Millennial Harbinger,* (1860), p. 151.
[40]A. L. McKinney, *Memoir of Eld. Isaac N. Walter* (Cincinnati,
1857), p. 368.
[41]Garrison and DeGroot, *op. cit.,* p. 285.
[42]*Millennial Harbinger,* (1839), p. 188. Woodson describes the
ministry of Marshall in more detail, and tells of the difficulties which
he experienced because of his acceptance of Campbell's views. *History of the Negro Church,* pp. 113-116.

spent the summers on the farm of his uncle, where he met Abram. As they worked together "along the interminable corn rows," the slave begged Williams to teach him to read. To this he consented, and the summer nights were spent in study. Williams says:

> Abram always kept stored away for me on those occasions baskets of the choicest fruits that he could find. The orchard, the garden and the vineyard, and even the dark, distant pawpaw woods, were laid under tribute for my enjoyment and reward. When these supplies failed I always had an ash-cake, with plenty of nice butter, and a liberal bowl of rich milk.[43]

Abram proved to be a "zealous and apt" student. Williams gave him a copy of the New Testament, and they read through the four Gospels. Soon Abram commenced teaching his fellow slaves in the cabin of his wife, who lived on another plantation. His reputation grew, as did his effectiveness as a preacher. Abram was a member of the Somerset Church, and that congregation encouraged him by granting him the use of the house to preach on Sunday afternoons. For many years after the Civil War, Abram Williams continued to preach. He was long a minister of the Negro Christian Church in Carlisle, Kentucky.[44]

To what extent did masters and slaves realize in the church their oneness in Christ? The records show that while many were conscious of the will of Christ for His church, they were not able to achieve a fellowship unalloyed by their social relationships. There was unity in song, prayer, and baptism. Both slave and master partook of one Lord's Supper, but there was usually some distinction in seating. Typical was Cane Ridge, where the relatively capacious balcony was reserved for the slaves and free Negroes. Among churches not possessing a balcony, a given section on the main floor was often occupied by the slaves.

---

[43]John A. Williams, *Reminiscences* (Cincinnati, 1898), pp. 161-164.
[44]*Ibid.*, pp. 170-171.

Such was the building of the Welche's Creek Church in North Carolina. It was weather boarded with pine boards one inch thick. There was only one window with glass in it. Primitive shutters closed the other apertures in unseasonable weather. The "pews" consisted of boards without backs, and light was supplied by tallow candles. The main part of the building, seating about one hundred and fifty was occupied by the whites. The "shed," which was an extension to the left of the "preacher's stand," seated about one hundred, and was reserved for the slaves. Certainly in this humble house masters enjoyed little pre-eminence over their servants.[45]

John Augustus Williams described the seating arrangements in Cambridge and Somerset, Kentucky. There the slaves sat together in designated portions of the "main room." Deacons of their own color were appointed to wait upon them. But not only were the Negroes segregated in the churches of Williams' youth; the "fair sisters" were likewise seated in a section reserved for them. This particularly struck Williams as "bad taste."[46]

In the Lord's Supper — that great sacrament of the church's unity — slaves and masters often found their richest fellowship. Through the "breaking of the bread" they affirmed in one act their common salvation. Indeed, Campbell affirmed that at the Lord's Table there were no masters or slaves.

Yet, even though men might sincerely confess that "*God is no respecter of persons*," it is exceedingly difficult to realize this fully in life. So it was that the thought forms of the social order often intruded into the very heart of worship. Some congregations did not serve the slaves until all the whites had partaken. Others had white deacons for the masters and black deacons for slaves. John Fee condemned these practices, saying:

---

[45]Ware, *North Carolina Disciples of Christ*, p. 255.
[46]Williams, *op. cit.*, p. 155.

> Slaves, though members with their masters, were
> not allowed to sit in the same part of the church
> house nor at the same time partake of the Lord's
> Supper with their white fellow Christians. The slave
> at this time sat in a gallery at the end of the church
> house, and when the white Christians had been
> served, one of the elders would say: "Now you black
> ones, if you wish to commune, come down."[47]

Describing the communion in the churches of his youth,
Williams also was impressed by the fact that the slaves partook of the Supper after their masters. "Such an arrangement," he said, "gave more emphasis to the social distinction than to the Christian oneness of which they sang."[48]

In the church at Welche's Creek, ceremonial footwashing
was observed in conjunction with the Lord's Supper. There
the congregation partook together of the communion, but
the "line" was drawn at the washing of feet. It was evidently
too much to expect a master to humble himself before his
slave in such a fashion. But who in this day is in a position
to judge?[49]

We have seen that slaves and masters both held membership in the same congregations among the churches of Christ
in the antebellum South. The development of distinctly
Negro congregations was not encouraged by these churches
to an extent comparable to the Methodists or Baptists. The
reasons for this difference are not clear, but it is probable
that the reformers' concern for Christian unity was an important factor.

Yet, although slaves and masters worshipped together,
the slave, by "the nature of his case," was limited in the extent of his participation in the life of the church. While
moral discipline was exercised toward both Negroes and
whites, the conditions of slave life gave more occasion for
such action regarding slaves than in the case of masters.

[47]*Autobiography* (Berea, Kentucky, 1891), p. 60. John Fee
[48]Williams, *op. cit.,* p. 155.
[49]Ware, *North Carolina Disciples of Christ,* p. 255.

The struggle of the churches against the fruits of the slavery system is here most evident.

It appears that the failure of successive emancipation efforts culminating in the Kentucky constitutional struggle of 1849, and the subsequent mass emigration of persons holding antislavery views, seriously weakened the witness of the churches. The power of the "system" appeared too great to be challenged successfully apart from a spiritual revival like that of 1801. Such an awakening was not to take place.

The church did not seem able to embody adequately the love of Christ. His "ministry of reconciliation" entrusted to it was compromised by the all-pervading spirit of a social system rooted in human alienation.

Therefore, in spite of the fact that in the church many masters and slaves found a deeply meaningful relationship, it was fraught with frustration. They were to learn that *where the Gospel of salvation was not allowed effectively to change their social relationship, the social relationship would compromise their reception of the joy of salvation.*

Thus we read of a portent of things to come in a minute from the church at Pleasant Grove, Kentucky:

> The church mett and organized on the 30th of Sept. 1854 and after worship proceeded to business. 1st the coloured portion of the church ask leave to buye a lott of ground to build a house to worship to themselves the church refuse the grant of priviledge but extend to them the use of the church to hold their meetings through the winter.
>
> G. T. Willcox MOD
> John W. Williamson, C. C.[50]

But such discontent was not only felt by slaves. Many whites who were devoted to the church were burdened by the incongruity of holding in bondage a person whom one confessed as "brother." Something had to give, and the ob-

---

[50]Pleasant Grove Minutes, September 30, 1854.

ligations of Christ's love made it clear that it was slavery which must yield. Yet, the power of the system was such that some felt it could only be overcome with the help of God.

The circuit rider, Elder Christy Sine, expressed it in a simple prayer:

> Lord when shall that happy time appear when the chains of bondage shall fall off — when those fetters shall be broken and universal liberty take place among the sons of Adam hasten the time Dear God in every land and among all people.[51]

If the "church of Christ on earth" is truly one, it must find a more adequate way to experience that unity, even amidst an alienated society. For this reason, the relation of the Gospel to the social order became a question of deep concern.

---

[51]Christy Sine, Journal (Unpublished; Library of Elon College, Elon College, N.C.).

IV

THE GOSPEL AND THE

SOCIAL ORDER

Ye are the salt of the earth: but if the salt have lost his savour, wherewith shall it be salted? It is thenceforth good for nothing, but to be cast out, and to be trodden under foot of men.

— JESUS

The Brotherhood of Thieves: or a True Picture of the American Church and Clergy.

— STEPHEN S. FOSTER

The bleeding captive plead his innocence, and pointed to Christianity who stood weeping at the cross. . . . But all was in vain. Slavery had stretched its dark wings of death over the land, the Church stood silently by — the priests prophesied falsely, and the people loved to have it so. Its throne is established, and now it reigns triumphant.

— HENRY GARNET

These statements merit earnest examination by the contemporary Christian. The first he will recognize as part of the Sermon on the Mount. The second is the title of a book by a bitter abolitionist critic of the last century. The third is taken from an address, "Call to Rebellion," delivered by a Negro Presbyterian pastor to the National Negro Convention in 1843.

Together they bring into poignant focus the issue which is central to our theme:

What is the relation of the Gospel to the social order?

How did the love of God expressed in Jesus speak to the issue of American slavery? How does it speak to the contemporary issue of race?

The church has often fallen under the judgment of the
very ideals it is charged to embody. The words of Jesus
with which He inaugurated His ministry also express His
intention for the church.

> The Spirit of the Lord is upon me, because he
> hath anointed me to preach the gospel to the poor;
> he hath sent me to heal the brokenhearted, to preach
> deliverance to the captives, and recovering of sight
> to the blind, to set at liberty them that are bruised,
>   To preach the acceptable year of the Lord (Luke
> 4:18, 19, KJV).

The modern attack upon the church for its apparent failure to live by the Gospel had its counterpart in the days of
the slavery controversy. Robert Owen, the famous social reformer and founder of the experimental communist society
of New Harmony, Indiana, antedated Karl Marx in his view
that religion was an "opiate," dulling men's social agony by
promising better things in life hereafter.[1]

Owen had developed a genuine social conscience although he was a wealthy owner of textile mills. In keeping
with his convictions he initiated advanced policies concerning working and living conditions in his Lanarkshire mills.
When these were successful he advocated their general
adoption throughout Britain, enforced by law. Parliament
proved unresponsive, however, and Owen therefore sought
the help of the established churches. When they refused to
become involved, he turned against Christianity, formulating
a declaration of religious principles which challenged the
relevance of both the Gospel and the church. In place of
the Christian concept of conversion, Owen substituted a

---

[1] A sympathetic treatment of these developments may be found in
George B. Lockwood, *The New Harmony Movement* (New York,
1905), p. 43 f.

rather thoroughgoing environmentalism. He would "give a new existence to man by surrounding him with superior circumstances only."[2]

Upon his arrival in America, Owen challenged any minister to debate the Christian religion. Alexander Campbell accepted the challenge, and the two met in Cincinnati in 1829.[3] Neither Owen nor Campbell had been satisfied with the existing order of things. Both were reformers. Both sought a new society, but they differed in their presuppositions and aims. Owen was an utopian, looking for a new world through scientific control of environment.

As an heir of the "tradition of Christ" Campbell looked for a new society in the form of the kingdom of God. This would be achieved not so much through scientific control of external environment as through reformation of the human heart. Spiritual reformation would lead to social change; but to attempt social change apart from spiritual reformation was inadequate because *every man was part of his fellows' "environment."*

The failure of New Harmony threw light upon the issue. For all the enthusiasm and talent of the famous "boatload of knowledge" which led in the settlement, the community did not fulfill the ideal envisioned for it. The gifted thinkers attracted to Owen's views could provide "superior circumstances," but not "superior circumstances *only*." Human nature caused other "circumstances" to appear — jealousy, selfishness, and greed — and the "noble experiment" failed.

But neither did Campbell's hope find fulfillment. The church's commitment to the "ministry of reconciliation" was not sufficient to overcome its own divisions — to say nothing of the alienation within society. Society could hardly be expected to embrace a way of life which the church itself did not exemplify.

Representing as it does man's scientific and spiritual

---

[2]*Ibid.*, p. 59.
[3]See Robert Owen and Alexander Campbell, *The Evidences of Christianity; A Debate* (Cincinnati: Standard Publishing Co., n.d.).

dilemma, the Campbell-Owen debate is very contemporary.

The bitter denunciations of Stephen S. Foster were hardly suited to the encouragement of the church in its task. He was in the habit of "non-violently" invading worship services of churches in the North to denounce members for their lack of involvement on behalf of the slave. More than twenty times he had been "thrown out," — acts which his biographer strangely considers to have been "violent responses" to his "non-violent" behavior.[4]

William Lloyd Garrison also stated his views in such a way as to make abolition of slavery the one cause by which everything else was judged. For this reason he was at times accused of being an "infidel." Garrison bitterly condemned the "mercenary and time-serving clergy," and berated the churches for not making the abolition of slavery their primary mission.

"NO UNION WITH SLAVEHOLDERS!"[5]   became Garrison's motto, and by that he meant no union, either political or religious. He vigorously castigated the political unionists who did not want to see the nation divided over slavery. But his most violent words were saved for those churches which refused to sever their relationship with members who held slaves. In Garrison's view, refusal to take positive action *against* slavery was tantamount to endorsing it. To such Christians he said, *"If your God allows men to be made beasts of, then your God is my Devil."*[6]   This simply

---

[4]Stephen S. Foster is not to be confused with Stephen C. Foster, the composer. See Oscar Sherwin, *Prophet of Liberty: The Life and Times of Wendell Phillips* (New York, 1958), pp. 76-78.

[5]*Liberator,* edited by William Lloyd Garrison (Boston, 1830-1865), XVII (1847), April 30. A recent treatment of Garrison is Eileen S. Kraditor, *Means and Ends in American Abolitionism: Garrison and His Critics on Strategy and Tactics, 1834-1850* (New York: Pantheon Books, 1968).

[6]Quoted in *Millennial Harbinger,* (1847), p. 112. For developments in Garrison's religious thought see Russell B. Nye, *William Lloyd Garrison and the Humanitarian Reformers* (Boston, 1955), pp. 136-138; also Ralph Korngold, *Two Friends of Man . . . William Lloyd Garrison and Wendell Phillips* (Boston, 1950).

meant that one was either a militant antislavery activist or he was not a Christian.

A more measured, but equally earnest, judgment was expressed by James G. Birney in his book, *The American Churches the Bulwarks of American Slavery*. Birney was editor of the *Philanthropist,* published in Cincinnati, where his office was destroyed by a mob in 1836. He was by temperament less volatile than Garrison or Foster, and by background was better qualified to understand the problems of slavery. He had himself made the pilgrimage from slaveholder to colonizationist to abolitionist — a pilgrimage which evidenced his sincerity.

Birney considered the churches "bulwarks" of slavery, not so much because there were among the clergy and laity those who *advocated* it, but because he believed the great majority of congregations were "shunning" the issue. Their plea that slavery was "a civil and political institution," that it "belonged to Caesar" and not to the church to abolish it, did not satisfy him.

Christians had a moral and ethical responsibility to lead the social order. The failure to act positively against the slavery system only served to perpetuate it, for *it removed from the struggle the strongest moral force in the land.*

Even if churches could not effect large scale change within society, Birney believed they did have the responsibility to discipline their own members. Therefore, any religious body which did not act for the removal of slavery within its own communion was without excuse.[7]

The bitter denunciations of men like Garrison and Foster, and the more moderate but equally telling thrusts of Birney, were a genuine source of concern to some abolitionists who were devoted to the church. B. U. Watkins wrote to John Boggs, editor of the antislavery *North-Western Chris-*

---

[7]An American (James G. Birney), *The American Churches the Bulwarks of American Slavery*, (Newburyport, 1842, 2nd American edition), p. 5. This was written and first published in England in 1840.

tian Magazine, expressing his sorrow that men outside the church "have sometimes understood the moral bearing of Christianity, better than Christians themselves." When "unbelievers" surpassed professed Christians in ethical sensitivity they could "challenge the moral code of Christianity, as greatly inferior to their own example."[8]

The agony of those who loved the church, but were dismayed by its apparent lack of social conscience, is revealed in the words of Jane C. McKeever:

> Tell it not among the scoffers of our holy religion, lest they rejoice — publish it not amongst the infidels, lest they triumph to hear that those who profess to take the Bible alone for their rule of faith and practice, and knowing that the Saviour has commanded them "to do to others as they would have others do to them," should be riveting the fetters of ignorance, oppression, and degradation upon those for whom Christ died.[9]

But what of the church? Were these criticisms justified? In what measure, and in what way did it fulfill its given role as mediator of the Gospel unto men whose lives were cursed by slavery? Any discriminating answer to these questions must recognize their great complexity. Men apparently of equal talent responded in different ways, just as they do today. In general, the problem of slavery was addressed from two major standpoints.

On one hand were those who believed the *primary* task of the church was to *proclaim* and *embody* the redeeming love of Christ, calling men into his fellowship through the Gospel. They learned from the New Testament that in this fellowship of the Spirit, entered through baptism and renewed in the Lord's Supper, human social distinctions are to be transcended by a common brotherhood — there is

---

[8]*North-Western Christian Magazine,* IV (1857), pp. 20, 21.

[9]*North-Western Christian Magazine,* I (1854), pp. 153, 154. Jane McKeever was a sister of Alexander Campbell.

neither Jew nor Greek, bond nor free (Gal. 3:28). The love of Christ shed abroad (Rom. 5:5) in men's hearts would transform their social relationships, constraining them to remove every form of injustice and inequity within their power. After all, while Paul sent the fugitive slave, Onesimus, back to Philemon, he reminded him that Onesimus had now become his "brother in the Lord" (Philem.).

In this view, social justice was a *consequent* of the Gospel. One ought not expect to harvest the fruit before the seed had been planted. The task of the church was to devote its energies to the planting of the seed — the Word of God. From this, it was believed, human equity and justice would follow. In this view, the Gospel was not an opiate dulling men's sensitivity to social injustice, but a creative power which was "perfectly adapted to the recovery and healing of the nations."[10]

To some moderns this confidence in the "Good News concerning Jesus" may seem idealistic or even escapist. But to these reformers it was a live option *if men took it seriously*. Obviously, proclamation of the Gospel *in word only* would have little effect (James 1:25 f.). But if its principles were embodied in persons its power would be released (Rom. 1:16). As W. K. Pendleton expressed it:

> We must have men to work out the good, and we are far from thinking that Christians should sit supinely by, and see the spirit of evil stalking in ruin over the fairest and brightest hopes, alike of civilization and religion.[11]

In short-term "solutions" Pendleton had little confidence. If those social injustices which were deeply rooted in the hearts of men were to be erased, "the morality of the Bible must become the moving power in the polity of the Land." This would only happen as the church "lifted up" the Christ.

---

[10]John Rogers, *The Biography of Elder J. T. Johnson* (Cincinnati, 1861), p. 66.

[11]*Millennial Harbinger*, (1860), pp. 171, 172.

To a significant number of concerned Christians this position was totally inadequate. It was too slow and indirect
in light of the rapidly developing crisis. It was not enough
that the church simply proclaim the Gospel, hoping that it
would bear fruit in due time. Christians were obliged to
cast themselves directly into the struggle for social justice
by every legitimate means. In the prophetic tradition the
church must declare the *meaning* of God's Word for contemporary society. But it must do more than *speak* — it must
live the Gospel. The church is called to *embody and exemplify in itself* the way of life it commends to the world.

Some Christian abolitionists went yet further. The
churches should cast their institutional power directly into
the struggle against slavery. The place to begin, they believed, was to excommunicate all those who held slaves, or
who were not *in opinion* strongly antislavery. Then, with a
united front the churches should seek the political power
necessary to break the hold which slavery had upon the
nation.

These activists could not abide gradualism or indirection,
for they felt time was "running out." Dr. Alexander Campbell, formerly a Senator from Ohio, wrote in 1835, "How
long," must the slaves bear their bonds? "They have waited
now more than half a century," he said, "and what has
been done?" He was convinced that each succeeding year
served to fasten slavery more securely upon the nation, and
that it would ere long be too late for emancipation to be
achieved peacefully. In very contemporary language he
called for action, "*Now*."[12]

With similar urgency, William Goodell, who styled himself an "independent Christian," appealed to the Christian
Anti-Slavery Convention meeting in Cincinnati in 1850, saying:

---

[12]*Christian Palladium,* edited by Joseph Badger; others (New York:
Union Mills, 1832-1861), IV (1835), p. 258. This was an official
publication of the "Christian Connection" in the East.

> If two hundred years of Christian (?) slavehold-
> ing does not suffice for us, and if eighteen years of
> unremitting and earnest testimony amid the thunder
> peals of divine Providence, (and while the nation is
> reeling to and fro, like a drunken man, under the
> tokens of divine displeasure,) be not *sufficient season
> of preliminary action,* what hope is there of a more
> "convenient season," and when will the time for
> vigorous and decisive Christian discipline arrive?[13]

Wendell Phillips expressed the impatience of many activists with programs of education as well as conversion. He
said:

> Our object is not to make every man a Christian
> or a Philosopher, but to induce everyone to aid in
> the abolition of slavery. We expect to accomplish
> our object long before the nation is made over into
> saints or elevated into philosophers.[14]

To the view that Christians ought not engage in such
political activism as petitioning legislative bodies, John Cur-
rier wrote from New England, "Pray tell us, when you have
shut up these avenues, how your *gospel law* is to be brought
to bear upon our afflicted fellows and brethren."[15]

Perhaps the complexity of this issue may best be viewed
through the intellectual pilgrimage of James A. Garfield.
When he was a lad on the Western Reserve, the congregation of which he was a member discussed their relation to
government and concluded that Christians "had no right to
engage in politics." It was, in Garfield's words, "like serving
two masters to participate in the affairs of government
which is point blank opposed to the Christian."[16]

During the same period he heard the abolitionist con-

---

[13]*Minutes of the Christian Anti-Slavery Convention of 1850,* (Cincinnati, 1850), p. 65.

[14]Sherwin, *op. cit.,* p. 269.

[15]*Christian Palladium,* VIII (1839), p. 248.

[16]Theodore C. Smith, *Life and Letters of James Abram Garfield*
(2 vols., New Haven, 1925), I, p. 39.

gressman, Joshua R. Giddings, and confided to his "Journal" his belief that the cause for which Giddings labored was "a carnal one."[17] Meanwhile, he read with approval eight essays (evidently by Campbell) on the subject of slavery and Christianity. These led him to conclude that the *"simple relation* of master and slave is NOT UNCHRISTIAN."[18]

Garfield was convinced that slavery would disappear in the course of time, perhaps by some natural process. While attending Western Eclectic Institute (Hiram) he was confirmed in this opinion by Professor Brainerd who concluded a lesson in geology with "an affectionate address" on "the *Geological Abolition of Slavery.*"[19]

Any who are prone to chuckle at such naiveté ought not forget that this is not the last time social thinkers have borrowed thought forms from the natural sciences. Such analogical reasoning may be found in Positivism, Social Darwinism, and in much contemporary sociological theory.

The question, of course, is whether such thinking is valid. What evidence was there that social processes follow geological patterns? Could men — can men — abdicate their responsibility for ethical social decision on the ground that "nature" will ultimately "solve" their problems through some strange, inexorable process called "progress"?

Furthermore, where did the *"simple relation* of master and slave" actually exist in real life? Campbell never defended the *system* of slavery on this ground, for he saw the system was very different from the theoretical relationship. Slavery was "that largest and blackest blot upon our national escutcheon, that many-headed monster, that Pandora's box, that bitter root, that blighting and blasting curse. . . ."[20] In 1832 he had prophetically declared:

---

[17]*Ibid.,* I, p. 39.

[18]Diary No. 1, Sunday, 29 September, 1850. Mss. Div., LC. Campbell had published a series of eight essays on the subject of slavery in the *Millennial Harbinger* during 1845.

[19]Diary No. 4, Friday, 2 November, 1855, Mss. Div., LC.

[20]*Millennial Harbinger,* (1832), p. 87.

> As sure as the Ohio winds its way to the Gulph
> of Mexico, will slavery desolate and blast our politi-
> cal existence, unless effectual measures be adopted
> to bring it to a close while it is in the power of the
> nation — while it is called today.[21]

The "simple relation" was one thing. The "system" was
quite another. Garfield was ultimately to confront these questions while pursuing his studies in Williams College. There
he determined that the "geological abolition" of slavery
was not enough. His prophetic heritage as a Christian asserted itself.

The turning point came one night when he heard an address by J. H. Patterson, an abolitionist editor from Kansas.
This man had been subjected to the violence of a proslavery
mob,[22] and his account of the experience powerfully moved
the future President.

Upon returning to his room that evening he confided to
his "Journal":

> At such hours as this I feel like throwing the
> whole current of my life into the work of opposing
> this great Evil — I don't know but the religion of
> Christ demands some such action.

> > "It needs a Daniel to translate the fire
> > That burns upon the walls at Washington
> > Where proud Belshazzar steeped in sin
> > Heeds not the fate that threatens to destroy
> > The mad assassins of our Liberty."[23]

So Garfield moved from a monastic isolationism through
a form of "social naturalism," to one in which he was convinced that the Christian should become prophetically involved in the issues of the day. Many others were to share
his pilgrimage.

---

[21]*Ibid.*, (1832), p. 88.
[22]Diary No. 4, Friday, 2 November, 1855. Mss. Div., LC.
[23]*Ibid.*, Friday, 2 November, 1855. Mss Div., LC.

The pulpit naturally reflected this struggle. Ought the
minister concentrate in proclaiming the "good news concerning Jesus," calling men to decision for Him? Or, should
he devote himself to declaring the way in which the teaching of Christ speaks to the social order? Ought he be content to voice to the world the faith of the congregation which
called him, even though that faith be limited? Or, should
he voice his understanding of the Word of God, letting it
judge both himself and his congregation? Should he elicit
from men their personal, ethical decision? Or should he attempt to mobilize the institutional power of the church in
the "good cause"?

Those familiar with the modern pulpit will immediately
sense the contemporary relevance of these questions. Some
churches both North and South, required their ministers to
hold the "correct" views of these matters. In 1860 Theobald
Miller wrote Garfield from Salem, Ohio, inviting him to
preach during a "protracted meeting." Miller was especially
anxious that Garfield come, for it was only "men of the right
stripe" who could be effective in Salem. The community
was solidly "Antislavery."[24]

Other preachers were also known for their antislavery
views. William D. Stone was both a minister and a "con-
ductor" of the "Underground Railroad." John Boggs praised
him as one who was "ready to live out Christianity every-
where and at all times." The constant subject of his private
and public conversation was abolition of slavery. Indeed,
when Boggs first met Stone he was singing a song about the
"Railroad":

> I'm on my way to Canada
> Where the colored man is free.[25]

---

[24]James A. Garfield Papers, 4PI2, June 5-December 21, 1860, no.
246. Mss. Div. LC.

[25]John Boggs, "Octogenarian Reminiscences, The Autobiography
of John Boggs," p. 114. Typewritten mss. prepared under supervision
of Cecil K. Thomas, Phillips University. Copy in Disciples of Christ
Historical Society, Nashville.

In Iowa, Elder Jonas Hartzell saturated his preaching with abolitionism. To him the question was simple: "If Jesus Christ was a slaveholder," then all Christians ought to be slaveholders. If Christ had no slaves, then Christians ought not to possess them. He failed to see why this should not settle the matter for anybody who professed the name of Jesus.[26]

In Kansas, Pardee Butler was twice nearly killed by proslavery mobs. On the first occasion they "rafted" him on the river, expecting him to drown. When he returned some months later he was nearly lynched. Only at the last minute was he "tarred and cottoned" instead, and ridden out of town.[27]

From Ladoga, Indiana, an "Honest Disciple" wrote John Boggs that "some of the brethren" refused to hear certain preachers because they were "preaching politics." "Honest Disciple" complained that the exhortation, "Do unto all men as you would they should do to you," was not "politics." This was, of course, the question.[28]

On the other hand, Elder John Winans wrote to Campbell that a couple had withdrawn from the church in Jamestown, Ohio, complaining that he was not "preaching the Gospel" because he did not preach against slavery. Winans was himself an antislavery man. However, he saw little point in preaching on the subject when no one in the congregation advocated the system, and there wasn't a "slaveholder living within sixty miles."[29]

When a society faces a critical ethico-social question, if the church is silent it is condemned as being irrelevant. But if it speaks, how can it avoid the charge that it is "meddling in politics," with the resultant rise of anticlericalism?

This issue of "political preaching" was debated by Rev.

---

[26]*North-Western Christian Magazine*, I (1854), pp. 260, 261.
[27]Rosetta B. Hastings, *Personal Recollections of Pardee Butler*, (Cincinnati, 1889), p. 108.
[28]*North-Western Christian Magazine*, IV (1857), p. 173.
[29]*Millennial Harbinger*, (1845), pp. 505-507.

Alfred Nevin and Jeremiah S. Black, Chief Justice of the
Supreme Court of Pennsylvania. Nevin claimed that political
and social issues were so closely entwined with religion
that it was impossible to "preach one without introducing
the other." Judge Black disagreed. "The vice of political
preaching was wholly unknown to the primitive Church,"
he said. This did not mean, however, that Christianity had
no relevance to social issues. Religion had power, but it was
to be found in the elevation of "the individuals of whom
society is composed."

Black sought to distinguish between the two approaches,
saying:

> A gospel preacher addresses the conscience of his
> hearers for the honest purpose of converting them
> from the error of their ways — a political preacher
> speaks to one community, one party, or one sect,
> and his theme is the wickedness of another. . . . Both
> classes of preachers frequently speak upon the same
> or similar subjects, but they do so with different ob-
> jects and aims.[30]

The *purpose* and the *approach* were with Judge Black the
distinguishing differences between "political preaching" and
"Gospel preaching." In his view, they both could address
the problem of slavery, but "political preaching" simply
served further to alienate men from one another. Only
when the Gospel is preached as a "ministry of reconciliation"
can it have *creative* social power.

So the issue was drawn concerning the relation of the
Gospel and the church to the social evil of slavery. Some
would concentrate the energies of the church upon proclamation of the Good News concerning Jesus Christ, trust-
ing in its "reflex light" to advance social justice. Others
would emphasize the meaning of that Good News for hu-

---

[30]Jeremiah S. Black, "Political Preaching," *Philadelphia Evening
Bulletin,* in Chauncy F. Black, *Essays and Speeches of Jeremiah S.
Black* (New York, 1886), pp. 69-71.

man relationships, actively cultivating its fruits in the social order. Some would limit social or political involvement to individual Christians, while others urged that the church use its institutional power to free the slave.

It is obvious that the church was limited in the degree to which it could influence the nation to abolish slavery. To seek control of a social order by strategic manipulation of the levers of power has at times been the choice of churches, as was the case in Calvin's Geneva. Yet, when the church behaves as a "pressure group," seeking to impose the "ethics of the Kingdom" upon an unconverted citizenry, its efforts have often been self-defeating. In the words of John Bright:

> A non-Christian world will not put into practice the ethics of Christ and cannot, for all our chiding, be made to do so. In a non-Christian world the teachings of Jesus are simply not "practical," as that world is quick to declare. To realize the ethics of the Kingdom it is first necessary that men submit to the rule of that Kingdom. . . .[31]

But this does not excuse the church from responsibility to seek social justice for all men. It is not the *aim* of the ecclesiastical pressure group which is wrong, but the *method*. The church is not called to "lord it over" men. Jesus specifically rejected such an approach (Matt. 23:11, 12). Rather, He sent the church into the world as a servant-community. Greatness would be determined by servant-hood.

For the church to be in the world as a pressure group is to be incapable of effecting genuine social change. Pressure groups exert influence externally, seeking by various means to manipulate behavior. But, as Reinhold Niebuhr has said, "Great social evils are corrected and social changes made,

---

[31]*The Kingdom of God* (Nashville: Abingdon, 1953), pp. 223, 224. For a classic treatment of alternative views see H. Richard Niebuhr, *Christ and Culture* (New York: Harper and Row, 1956).

on the whole, by implicit rather than explicit processes."[32]

It is the role of the servant-community to work "implicitly," through the witness of testimony and example to *win* men to a "more excellent way." As Niebuhr noted, the "concept of human rights" is impotent "if the community does not have the moral and cultural resources to comprehend it."[33] It is the task of the church to provide these resources.

But if the church could not be held responsible for the behavior of a non-Christian slaveholder, it *was* responsible for its own life. Birney was right: the church was judged by its failure to embody the Gospel in its corporate life. It was failing to exemplify before men what God sought for all in His kingdom. This failure tended to confirm social injustice.

The spirit of alienation was all too prevalent in the church. The issue was a dynamic one, concerning the flow of power — not simply political power, but spiritual. It may be stated simply:

> Shall the spirit of *alienation* flow from the world through the church, unto the compromise of the radical demands of the Gospel?

Or:

> Shall the spirit of *reconciliation* flow from the Gospel through the church, unto the reformation of society?

Yet, while the issue is stated simply, the dynamics are complex.

How, for example, could the church realize the divine fiat that there is "neither bond nor free?" In what way was a slave not a slave at the Lord's Table, or the master not a master? Could their brotherhood be *real* if it only existed at that brief moment? If more was demanded by the Gospel,

---

[32]*Pious and Secular America* (New York: Scribner's, 1958), p. 81.
[33]*Ibid.,* pp. 80, 81.

if *all* of life was involved, how was brotherhood to speak to the slave-master relationship?

Brotherhood declared in no uncertain terms, *Do what love requires.* But what was one to do if law or custom hindered or forbade what love required? Should one who would live by love condition his behavior to an unjust "situation"? Or, does love require him to break the situation, or be broken by it? Which was the way of the Cross?

These were not mere theoretical questions. The Christian master confronted by laws restricting the education or emancipation of his slaves had to choose whether to live within the law, or to "do what love required." The Christian slave had a like choice, only from a different position.

But master and slave were not alone in facing this issue. The Fugitive Slave Law was to create a crisis of conscience for Christians in the North, bringing many who had been far removed from the system of slavery to their "moment of truth."

The Gospel is related to the social order in the Cross of Christ. There, the spirit of alienation was confronted by the spirit of reconciliation. There, love met law, suffered under it, and triumphed over it.

But how is this mystery to be made socially dynamic by those who follow Jesus? The Fugitive Slave Law was to demand an answer to this question.

V
CRISIS OF CONSCIENCE

When the unity of society and the values of social order are found in conflict with the conscience of the Christian citizen, what is he to do? Is an "unjust law" to be disobeyed, and the consequence of that disobedience to be suffered? Or should one obey on the ground that the individual is not responsible for the "immoral laws" which a society may invoke?

How do these questions relate to the type of government under which the citizen lives? Is the Christian living within a representative democracy obliged to act differently toward "unjust laws" than one living under a dictatorship such as that of Hitler?[1] Is disobedience to law justified when the courts are open and legislatures are freely elected?

Is there a moral difference between violent obstruction of law and "civil disobedience"? Or, again, is the Christian justified in passively countenancing social injustice on the ground that "the Gospel has nothing to do with politics?"

The contemporary racial crisis confronts many citizens with such questions. Their complexity is revealed in the re-

---

[1]This was a critical aspect of the issue facing the martyred German pastor, Dietrich Bonhoeffer, when he joined in a plot against Hitler. See *The Way To Freedom, Letters, Lectures and Notes 1935-1939*, ed. by Edwin H. Robertson, trans. by Edwin H. Robertson and John Bowden (New York: Harper and Row, 1966), pp. 147-202. As to civil disobedience in a democratic society, see Martin Luther King, Jr., "Letter From a Birmingham Jail," in *Why We Can't Wait* (New York: Harper and Row, 1964).

cent report of the National Commission on the Causes and Prevention of Violence. This panel of eminent political, judicial, and religious leaders divided over the issue by a vote of seven to six. The majority wrote, "In our democratic society, lawlessness cannot be justified on the grounds of individual belief." The minority dissented, affirming the right of conscience to engage in "civil disobedience." If the "experts" cannot agree, what hope is there that the common man can understand?

The problem of "moral man and immoral society" has a long history.[2] Each generation seems to present the issue in different form, but with similar substance. Forms of dissent popularized by Ghandi have been adopted throughout the world, although it is perhaps not accidental that they are more effective in democratically oriented societies than in totalitarian systems.

It is significant that the division within the Commission on Violence had to do largely with the problem of racial justice. It was not a simple, theoretical question. The "long hot summers" of the last several years provided a poignant context within which the Commission deliberated. In like manner circumstances condition the thinking of every citizen, and in some way may prejudice his answer to the above questions before he has heard the "whole story."

For this reason, it is helpful to look to history, to former manifestations of the problem. These may be viewed (hopefully) with less passion and prejudice. Such a crisis of conscience was occasioned by the Fugitive Slave Law. Certainly, in the United States there has never been a more agonizing issue confronting Christian citizens than this law. Perhaps from it we may learn.

The new Fugitive Slave Act was passed by Congress on September 12, 1850. This law was part of a larger "Com-

---

[2]For a classic treatment of this problem see Reinhold Niebuhr, *Moral Man and Immoral Society* (New York: Scribner's, 1932).

promise," and amended the original law of 1793.[3]

Under provisions of the new Act, all cases involving fugitive slaves were placed under exclusive Federal control. Special United States Commissioners were empowered to issue warrants for the arrest of fugitives and after a summary hearing, to provide for their return to their masters. A simple affidavit by a claimant was considered to be sufficient evidence of ownership, while the testimony of a Negro claiming to be free was not admissible in any legal proceedings. Neither was a Negro claimed as a fugitive privileged to have trial by jury.

Violently condemned in the North was that portion of the Act which authorized a commissioner to receive a fee of ten dollars should certification of ownership be granted, but of only five dollars if it was refused. It was asserted that this weighted the scales against the Negro. Any federal marshal was liable to a fine of one thousand dollars for failure to execute a warrant, or could be sued for the value of a slave if he escaped through negligence of the marshal.

The Law likewise provided that any citizen who prevented the arrest of a fugitive, aided in his rescue, or concealed him from officials was subject to a fine of one thousand dollars, and imprisonment for six months. He was further liable to damages of one thousand dollars for each fugitive "lost" through such action.

These provisions confronted the antislavery Christian with a problem at once simple and complex. The Scripture

---

[3]The "Compromise of 1850" consisted of six bills: Texas bill (August 9); New Mexico bill (August 15); California bill (September 7); Utah bill (September 9); Fugitive Slave bill (September 12); District of Columbia slave-trade bill (September 14). The debate was one of great feeling, including the presentation of Henry Clay's original plan, and addresses by Calhoun, Webster, and Seward. *House and Senate Journals*, 31st Congress, 1st Session; William MacDonald, *Select Documents of the United States, 1776-1861* (revised edition, New York, 1905), nos. 78-83; Arthur M. Schlesinger, Jr., *Age of Jackson* (New York, 1945), chap. XXXIV; Theodore C. Smith, *Parties and Slavery* (New York, 1906), p. 14 f.

enjoined him to "be subject unto the higher powers."[4] But what should one do when the "powers" commanded that which conscience forbade?[5]

A gradual divergence of interest and thought-life had meanwhile developed between North and South. The natural result of this cultural schism was that what was considered perfectly legitimate by many citizens in one section became revolting to many in another. This divergence was accelerated by writers in both North and South who manifested little desire to understand one another.[6]

Highly offensive to most people in the North were advertisements for runaway slaves, which appeared with increasing regularity in Southern newspapers. Typical of these notices is the following, which appeared in the *Kentucky Yoeman*. Accompanied by a picture of a fugitive, it read:

---

[4]Romans 13:1.

[5]The Fugitive Slave Act was signed by President Fillmore on September 18, 1850. It "opened a new era in the Abolition movement, an era in which non-resistance had no place." Oscar Sherwin, *Prophet of Liberty: The Life and Times of Wendell Phillips*, p. 223. One can therefore see why it constituted an especially difficult problem to many Christians.

[6]*American Slavery As It Is*, by Theodore D. Weld and his wife Angelina Grimke Weld, was published in 1839. It consisted of extracts from Southern newspapers and the testimony of antislavery visitors to the South. *Uncle Tom's Cabin*, by Harriet Beecher Stowe, was inspired by the Fugitive Slave Law, and published in 1852. It probably exerted more influence than any other single work, being dramatized as well as printed. *The Constitution a Pro-Slavery Compact*, was written by Wendell Phillips in 1845, advocating "NO UNION WITH SLAVEHOLDERS." *The Pro-Slavery Argument*, by William Harper, Thomas R. Dew and James H. Hammond, appeared in 1852, arguing that slavery was a positive good. *Sociology for the South; or, the Failure of Free Society* (1854), and *Cannibals All! or, Slaves Without Masters* (1857), both written by "the propagandist of the Old South," George Fitzhugh, defended slavery by attacking free labor. Culminating the South's apology was *Cotton is King*, edited by E. H. Elliott (1860). Contributors were A. T. Bledsoe and David Christy, on economics; Thornton Stringfellow, the Bible argument; J. H. Hammond, and Chancellor Harper, social considerations; S. A. Cartwright; ethnological theory.

$100 REWARD

RAN AWAY from the subscriber, living in Frankfort a negro fellow by the name of

ANTHONY.

He is about 5 feet 10 or 11 inches in height, a stout, heavy negro, and very black; has a bushy head of wool; in front of the lower jaw he has no teeth; his feet have been frost-bitten, in consequence of which he has lost the nail off one of his big toes, and part of the other. If caught in the county, I will give ten dollars if delivered to me; out of the county, twenty dollars; and if taken out of the State and delivered to me, I will give the above reward.

PATRICK MAJOR

August 8th, 1844[7]

Another such notice, accompanied by the same picture indicates the widespread efforts which were made to recapture fugitives, for this master advertised in the *Yoeman,* although he lived in Alabama.

$100 REWARD!

I have lost a Negro man, a slave, by the name of Bill, formerly belonging to William Robertson, of Cox county, Tennessee. Said boy escaped the jail of Cox county, and was apprehended in Letcher county, Ky., and broke that jail, and was aiming for the Ohio. The said boy is about 26 years old; 5 feet 2 inches high, and a bright mulatto; speaks quick and sharp; very bow-legged; wears whiskers to a point at the chin; had on when left here, brown linsey pants, a short coat, and a fur cap. He professes to be a barber.

I will give $50 reward for the apprehension of said boy in Kentucky or Virginia; the sum of $100 if taken in Ohio; and $25 in Tennessee, or in any

[7]*Kentucky Yoeman,* V (1844), no. 23.

other State, and will pay all reasonable charges, if
taken and secured so I get him.

My residence is in Selma, Dallas county, Ala.

JEREMIAH JOHNSON

Nov. 14th, 1844[8]

It is of interest that Bacon College (a predecessor of
Transylvania), regularly advertised in the *Yoeman,* where
on more than one occasion its notice appeared next to a
fugitive slave advertisement. This fact seemed to cause no
stir of feeling among the churches in Kentucky which supported the College.

The plight of many fugitives elicited strong public sympathy
in the North. Newspapers gave wide coverage to legal proceedings against escaped slaves, and recorded with favor
occasions when citizens combined to frustrate the due process of law.[9] Although some fugitives were criminals, the
antislavery Northerner tended to idealize them all. This
attitude was immeasurably strengthened by publication of
Uncle Tom's Cabin.

There is little question that John Boggs aroused the feelings of many Disciples in Indiana and Ohio when he published the account of nine who were captured in Cincinnati
in 1854.

Boggs vividly described the scene:

> The leader of the party was an old man, whose
> head was frosted by some sixty winters. He was the
> husband of one of the women, and the father of

---

[8]*Ibid.,* no. 41.

[9]A fugitive, Anthony Burns, was captured in Boston in June, 1854.
Local opposition to the operation of the law was so great that President Pierce sent a Federal vessel to carry Burns back to his master
in Virginia. Corydon Fuller, an intimate friend of James A. Garfield,
said that this action contributed greatly to the crystallization of public sentiment into a "hatred of the infamous institution which demanded such shameful services of those who had supposed themselves
freedmen." Corydon Fuller, *Reminiscences of James A. Garfield*
(Cincinnati, 1887), p. 165.

some of the children. We saw him at the court-
room during his trial and that of his comrades. His
whole exterior gave the most unequivocal evidence
that his life had been one of toil and hardship, —
still he had the appearance of a man. There was
intelligence in his eye, and although he had been
defeated in his well-meant efforts to obtain a boon
of liberty, and was surrounded by his enemies, he
looked calmly on at the actions of those who were
busily co-operating with the petty tyrant who claimed
him as his property, to hasten him back to the land
of bondage, and cruelty, and tears. We could not
but contrast in our mind the calmness, dignity, and
christian resignation depicted on the countenance of
the patriarch "Shaderech," with that of the bloated,
debauched, and besotted appearance of some, and
the miserly, hard-fisted, flint-skinning looks of the
rest of the gang of slave-owners and slave-catchers
by whom he was almost surrounded.[10]

These slaves, said Boggs, were being tried for the "same
crime that so darkened the escutcheon of our forefathers
. . . the crime of *loving* LIBERTY and *hating* SLAVERY."
When he later learned that this slave family had been separated through sale to different masters, Boggs bitterly remarked that "the strongest evidence we can give of our
christian character is our advocacy of, and submission to,
this 'fugitive law.' "[11]

The multiplication of such instances left few in the North
untouched by the Fugitive Slave Law. Time and again,
public opinion was inflamed by the actions of federal officers
or their cohorts in attempting to return fugitives to their masters.[12]

---

[10]*North-Western Christian Magazine,* I (1854), p. 18.

[11]*Ibid.,* I (1854), p. 18.

[12]A famous instance was the "Oberlin-Wellington" rescue in which
students of Oberlin College joined with local citizens to rescue a
fugitive by force. They were prosecuted by the Federal Government, but public opinion forced the officials to drop the matter.
See Marion G. McDougall, *Fugitive Slaves, 1619-1865* (Boston,
1891), chaps. iii, iv. Oberlin quite naturally became a "station" on

Confronted by such situations, Christians in the North tended to take two major positions. On one hand were those who advocated obedience to the law "for the Lord's sake," while attempting to get it constitutionally repealed. This was the view of Alexander Campbell. On the other hand were many such as John Boggs, Isaac Errett, and Ovid Butler, who refused obedience to the law and expressed willingness to suffer its penalty rather than to comply.

Those who refused to obey the Fugitive Slave Law did so on the basis of a "Higher Law," whether that "Law" were interpreted in theistic or in humanistic terms. Boggs appealed to the theistic principle when he reminded the owners of "Shederech," "There is a higher court than any in this city, or in this State, or even in these United States." Before it they would one day themselves be tried. "Although you may now treat with scorn and derision the *higher law,*" he said, "still it is the law by which we shall all be judged."[13]

Sermons were preached in pulpits throughout the land, espousing the "Higher Law." Such was the message delivered by Rev. Nathaniel Colver, Pastor of the Tremont Street Church in Boston, entitled, "The Fugitive Slave Bill; or, God's Laws Paramount to the Laws of Man." Under his influence, Colver's congregation had resolved, "That as disciples of Christ, and members of his church, we ought not, we cannot, and as we fear God, we will not, render obedience to the said law." The position of this congregation was widely shared in New England.

Colver was himself even more violent in his denunciation, saying in his sermon:

---

the Underground Railroad. Albert B. Hart, *Slavery and Abolition,* p. 193.

When Frederick Douglass visited New Bedford, Massachusetts, he was told that a "would-be Judas," who was about to report a fugitive slave to the authorities, was nearly killed in the Third Christian Church (colored) of that city. *Life and Times of Frederick Douglass,* pp. 237, 238.

[13]*North-Western Christian Magazine,* I (1854), p. 18 f.

This law should be abhorred and trampled under
foot by every man, because it enjoins the commission of one of the blackest crimes specified in the
divine catelogue — a crime classified by an inspired
apostle with murderers of fathers, murderers of
mothers — MAN-STEALER.[14]

The Christian Church in Berrien, Michigan, circulated a
series of resolutions which are noteworthy not only for
their firmness and gentleness, but for their keen perception
of the problem. This congregation declared:

1. That Christians are required by their Lord and
Master to yield a cheerful obedience to the "powers
that be," provided their laws do not contravene the
"higher law."
2. That the Fugitive Slave Law, passed by Congress at its last session, *does,* obviously conflict with
the Divine Law in several particulars.
3. That it is not only *not* the duty of Christians
to obey the said law, but a positive dereliction of
duty to their Divine Master, to regard it as of any
authority over them.
4. That choosing to "obey God rather than man,"
we will not assist the master in recapturing "the servant that has escaped from his master," but will
feed the poor panting fugitive, and point him to the
North Star, abiding the penalty of the law.
5. That we have long borne with slavery, for the
sake of the Union, as Christians ought to do; but
when called upon to aid and abet in perpetuating
the institution, we beg to be excused.
6. That as citizens of the United States, we will
petition our National Legislature for the immediate

[14]*Millennial Harbinger,* (1851), pp. 427, 428. The influential Boston minister, Theodore Parker, said of the Fugitive Slave Law, "I
say solemnly that I will do all in my power to rescue any fugitive
slave from the hands of any officer who attempts to return him to
bondage." Theodore Parker, *Speeches, Addresses, and Occasional
Sermons* (Boston, 1860), III, p. 154. Parker fulfilled this vow by
aiding in the attempt to free Anthony Burns in 1854. He was also
implicated in John Brown's raid. Henry S. Commager, *Theodore
Parker* (Boston, 1936), pp. 232 f., 250 f.

and unconditional repeal of this oppressive law, so
very repugnant to . . . liberty of conscience.

7. That we will discountenance all *violent* measures of opposition to the said law, or to any other,
but will pray for our rulers, and suffer persecution
at their hands with patience and forbearance, giving
glory to the Lord of all.[15]

The circulation of the "Berrien Resolves" had considerable
influence upon Christian churches north of the Ohio. Many
of their members had engaged in agonizing "soul searching"
because of the provisions of the Law. Ovid Butler (after
whom Butler University is named) wrote Campbell from
Indianapolis, expressing his sorrow that conscience should
require him to differ with the reformer. While he had not
formerly heard of the Berrien congregation, he felt they
truly expressed his convictions.

Butler objected to the Law on constitutional grounds,
"both in its principle and in its provisions." But he had
stronger and deeper objections than this, for "as a Disciple
of Jesus," he was constrained to regard its provisions as contrary to all principles of humanity, and in violation of "the
statutes and institutes of the Lord Christ." This was a decision of his conscience, and conscience was of necessity a
man's final tribunal.

Butler wrote that if anyone could show him how a Christian could conscientiously obey the Law, it would "remove
a weight of apprehension — of even dread" — which rested
upon him. Failing that, he could only pray that "the cross"
would be removed and that no demand should be made of
him to render obedience to the law.[16]

In this view, Butler was joined by the gifted minister and
editor, Isaac Errett. Errett was a close friend of Judge
Leicester King, vice-presidential candidate of the Liberty

---

[15]*Millennial Harbinger,* (1851), p. 172.
[16]*Ibid.,* (1851), pp. 433, 434.

Party.[17] Preaching on the "Design of Civil Government," Errett affirmed that when a law of man contravenes the law of God, the Christian has no choice but to obey God. Viewing the long series of extra-legal actions which had been taken in the South against antislavery men — some of which involved violence — Errett asked, "Why all this alarm *now*, when there is a simple refusal, on the part of many conscientious persons in the north, to obey what they regard as *unrighteous* requirements?"[18]

There was, of course, a difference between "simple refusal" to obey the Fugitive Slave Law, and active efforts to frustrate its intention. Yet, passive refusal to obey, and active endeavors to block fulfillment were both justified in the name of the "higher law." While the Berrien congregation had repudiated violence, Errett praised certain citizens of Philadelphia and Buffalo who had rescued Negro freemen from "slavecatchers," justifying their actions through appeal to the "court of conscience."[19]

---

[17]Leicester King was an elder of the Church of Christ in Warren. He was a member of the Ohio Senate from 1833-1838; president of the Ohio Anti-Slavery Society; vice-presidential candidate of the Liberty Party in 1847, from which nomination he withdrew in favor of the Van Buren ticket. Theodore C. Smith, *The Liberty and Free Soil Parties* (New York, 1897), pp. 85-116; Jesse Macy, *Anti-Slavery Crusade* (New Haven, 1919), pp. 91-95; Herbert A. Donovan, *The Barnburners* (New York, 1925), pp. 89-101; Glyndon G. Van Deusen, *The Jacksonian Era* (New York, 1959), pp. 257-259.

[18]The events to which Errett evidently refers were common knowledge. A number of abolitionist editors had suffered the loss of their presses, including James G. Birney, editor of the *Philanthropist*, published in Cincinnati, who barely escaped death when the office of the paper was destroyed by a mob in 1836. J. H. Patterson of Kansas and Cassius M. Clay of Kentucky were similarly treated.

The specific reference here is evidently to Elijah P. Lovejoy, editor of the *Observer*, an abolition paper in St. Louis. Driven to Alton, Illinois, for condemning the burning of a Negro at the stake, he twice saw his press destroyed. On November 7, 1837 a mob attacked his office. Lovejoy returned the fire, and was himself killed. Hart, *Slavery and Abolition*, p. 248; Carl R. Fish, *The Rise of the Common Man, 1830-1850* (New York: 1929), p. 279; Edward Beecher, *Narrative of the Riots at Alton* (1838).

[19]*Millennial Harbinger*, (1851), pp. 623-627, 631.

The religious overtones of the "higher law" also had their political counterpart. The great debate over the Compromise of 1850 brought Daniel Webster and William Seward into direct conflict concerning the subject. Seward said:

> The Constitution regulates our stewardship; the Constitution devotes the domain to Union, to justice, to defence, to welfare, and to liberty.
> But there is a *higher law than the Constitution* which regulates our authority over the domain, and devotes it to the same noble purposes. . . .[20]

This address was widely applauded by Christians in New England. A. M. Averill wrote to the *Christian Palladium* to praise Seward's enunciation of the "higher law." "It is the Empire Speech," he declared, "for it lays down principles that are as broad and deep as the Kingdom of God." Averill liked such "universal men," who bowed before the majesty of a law that was universal and eternal.[21]

In stark contrast, like many of his fellow-citizens, Averill castigated the famous Seventh of March Speech of Daniel Webster. Webster denied that a man was "at liberty to set up, or affect to set up his own conscience above the law." The nation could never survive a general application of the principle. Once the Constitution was set aside in the name of "higher law," social chaos would be the inevitable result.

Averill considered Webster "recreant" in assuming such a position. He had betrayed not only the citizens who had "delighted to honor" him, but had in effect thrown his great influence on the side of "oppression." Whittier's poem,

---

[20]Seward's defense of the principle of "higher law" may be found in his *Works*, ed. by George E. Baker (5 vols., Boston, 1853), I, pp. 66, 74.

Dwight L. Dumond notes Birney's early contribution to the idea of *"higher law"* in his *Antislavery Origins of the Civil War in the United States* (Ann Arbor, 1939), p. 99.

[21]*Christian Palladium*, XIX (1850), p. 73.

"Ichabod," well represented the sentiments of citizens such as Averill.[22]

As one traces these developments, he may well sympathize with the advocates of the "court of conscience." However, in application the principle was not as simple as it might first appear. There was an ambiguity in the concept of "higher law" which severely limited its value as a creative social force.

What *did* it really mean? Men such as John Boggs identified the "higher law" with the ethic of the Bible, and the "higher court" as the last judgment. Others attached to the principle a mystical element, subjective in nature, and quite separate from either the Bible or the Constitution. It might be the voice of a "Divinity within" each individual, or the voice of an "enlightened humanity." Some attempted a synthesis of natural rights and divine precepts.[23] Whatever its principle, the "higher law" tended to be self-justifying, and was often accompanied by strong emotional overtones.

It is not surprising, therefore, to find that the "higher law" as advocated in the North, had its southern counterpart. Tolbert Fanning, President of Franklin College, in Nashville, expressed his concern that such an idea had become so popular. It was preached from the pulpits, taught "in the Sunday school, in the steam boat, the railroad car, in the family, in the street." He considered it dangerous because it was evidently "all things to all men." Fanning said it was variously defined as "a power in the human soul, — called 'the divine spark' — 'the divinity within,' 'reason,' 'in-

---

[22]Whittier's famous poem, "Ichabod" was occasioned by Webster's supposed betrayal. Theodore C. Smith, *Parties and Slavery 1850-1859* (New York, 1906), p. 17.

[23]See the analysis of William Hosmer's synthesis of natural rights and divine precepts in Russel B. Nye, *Fettered Freedom, Civil Liberties and the Slavery Controversy, 1830-1860* (East Lansing, 1949), p. 194.

tuition,' 'conscience,' 'the moral sense.' "[24]

This ambiguity concerned the educator because its application to the social or religious order could only bring schism and discord. He observed:

> When the world fancies that there is another rule
> of right than the Bible, — that each mortal carries
> in his heart a guiding divinity — a higher law, —
> there is no common bond to bind humanity to-
> gether.[25]

Fanning illustrated his concern by noting that where the abolitionist invoked a private, subjective "higher law" to set at naught the Fugitive Slave Law, some southerners used a similar "higher law" to defend it. Already he had read arguments asserting that slavery was "absolutely right," "measured by the same higher law rule, equally odious." He felt for this reason that appeals based on such a principle could only result in "great mischief."[26]

For similar reasons, Justice Jeremiah S. Black also opposed the concept of "higher law." Speaking in Philadelphia, he declared that the "higher law" was a "code unrevealed, unwritten, and undefined." As such, it was the enemy of free men and institutions. Like the jealous king, it would "bear no brother near the throne." Its mission was to tread down whatever opposed it. In every age and in all countries, it had been intolerant and dogmatic. Black said, "It disdains all compromise, carries no olive branch — it takes both hands to wield the merciless sword."

For these reasons Justice Black declared that the nation

---

[24]*Gospel Advocate,* VII (1861), p. 65-70. (This periodical was edited by Tolbert Fanning and others, and published in Nashville, 1855-.)

[25]*Ibid.,* VII (1861), p. 65-70.

[26]An early application of the "higher law" principle was the action of Postmaster Amos Kendall when he refused to enforce delivery of "incendiary" publications in the South. A large shipment of such material had been burned in Charleston in 1835. Kendall acknowledged one's obligation to law, but said citizens owed "a higher one" to the communities in which they lived. Macy, *Anti-Slavery Crusade,* pp. 75, 76.

could not live by the Constitution and a "higher law" at the same time. "Anarchy, spoliation and bloodshed, conflagration, terror and tears," would "come in the place of Government and law."[27]

With this general view, Alexander Campbell agreed. He deeply regretted the intemperate outbursts and recriminations which citizens levelled at one another. He was yet more concerned by the actions of some religious groups, in which disobedience to the Fugitive Slave Law was advocated, even to the point of violence. This kind of behavior might have been expected of those who were not "well informed either on the Constitution of the United States or on that of Christ's Kingdom." But he failed to understand how "any one well-instructed in the Christian religion" could recommend violence or insubordination to a law which had been passed by a Congress which simply represented the will of the "sovereign people."[28]

American Christians, in Campbell's view, had other recourse than violence. The courts were open, and elections were free. He feared for the future of representative government if men in the name of "higher law" set aside the social compact. Christians had been enjoined "for the Lord's sake," to submit themselves to every "ordinance of men." This was especially so in a country where citizens possessed the constitutional right to reform laws which were considered "unjust."[29]

So the issues were drawn, and hundreds in both North and South, confronted by the Fugitive Slave Law, experienced the crisis of conscience. The fact that men of high repute differed concerning the proper response the Christian should make evidenced the complexity of the problem. As Campbell said, "More light is wanting somewhere."[30]

---

[27]Jeremiah S. Black, "Philadelphia Speech," in C. F. Black, *Essays and Speeches of Jeremiah S. Black*, p. 6.
[28]*Millennial Harbinger*, (1851), pp. 27-29.
[29]*Ibid.*, (1851), pp. 31, 32.
[30]*Ibid.*, (1851), p. 172 f.

The critical factor in the concept of "higher law" was the ethical criterion which one used as a basis of judgment. "Con-science" is a "knowing-with" — a "knowing with reference to something." The "something," or point of reference which one chooses is critical to the authentic role of conscience. Boggs' description of the proceedings in Cincinnati made it obvious that he thought and acted on a very different set of presuppositions than did the "slavecatchers" he despised. Their "higher law" — their theoretical justification — was the depersonalization of the slave. He was a "thing," a "chattel," a piece of property to be owned, used, and disposed of at will. A person's right to own another as property was greater than the other's right to be treated as a person. The right to recover one's property was greater than a slave's right to be free.

Boggs' "higher law" was the concept of the "equality of all men before God," and the mandate to love one's neighbor as oneself. On the basis of such presuppositions, he believed, one man could not in justice hold property in another. Neither could he live by the "Golden Rule" while returning a fugitive to bondage.

To see the fugitive as a person of worth — a person for whom Christ also died — was to affect profoundly one's view of a law which treated him as a thing. Many believed such a law was on its very face impious and unjust. If the ruler was indeed, "a minister of God to thee for good" (Rom. 13:4, ASV), the Fugitive Slave Law represented the prostitution of divinely given authority. Therefore the Christian citizen was no longer obliged to obey it. Some believed it was to be positively frustrated by every means at their disposal.

The rule of law was not relevant to one whose sympathies were profoundly moved by the sight of a Federal Marshal accompanied by a motley band of slave catchers leading a fugitive back to bondage. Who could wait for the odious law to be repealed? What prospect was there that the balance of political power would so change as to permit its repeal?

Was the Federal Union so important that countless fugitive slaves, and even some Negro freemen, must be sacrificed? Was the law to be tolerated when it stood on the side of inhumanity? No! thundered hundreds of voices in the North.

Yet, leaders such as Campbell saw the problem was not so simple as it might first appear. If the Federal Union were dissolved, what would happen to the millions of slaves still in bondage? If an "unjust" law were to be disobeyed by the "just," who could expect a "just" law to be obeyed by the "unjust?" What assurance was there that in setting aside the rule of law in order to obviate one "unjust" law, a flood of lawlessness would not inundate the nation and leave multitudes of the innocent to suffer?

Confounded by these paradoxes, many made no courageous decision — whether to obey or to disobey the law (and in some areas it took more courage to obey while seeking reform, than to disobey). Some simply chose to "go along" with whatever sentiment prevailed around them as an escape from the complexities of conscience and the responsibility of moral decision.

Dietrich Bonhoeffer was a century later to describe this choice when he wrote from a Nazi prison:

> Lonely, the man of "conscience" resists the superior force of the situation which demands a decision. But the extent of the conflicts in which he has to make a choice, guided and supported by nothing except his own conscience, tears him to pieces. The innumerable honorable and seductive disguises in which evil approaches him make his conscience fearful and uncertain, until he is finally satisfied with having a salved conscience instead of a good one, until he therefore deceives his own conscience in order not to despair. For the man whose only support is his conscience can never grasp the fact that a bad conscience can be stronger and more healthy than a deceived one.[31]

---

[31] *I Loved This People,* trans. by Keith R. Crim (Richmond, Va.: John Knox Press, 1966), pp. 19, 20.

Many who struggled against the Fugitive Slave Law were motivated by humanistic rather than Biblical concerns. Together, humanist and Christian shared common convictions concerning the worth and dignity of the individual. But the Christian's understanding was informed by the Cross of Jesus, and in that it was unique. In the Cross man's worth was affirmed even in his sin, for Christ "died for all." "The mystery of iniquity" was, indeed, at work in the world (II Thess. 2:7, KJV), and law was susceptible to its influence. Even the best law was limited in what it could do to ameliorate the conditions of human bondage, for law itself is only effective as it reflects the "spirit of the age." Therefore, men could only expect law to accomplish the elevation of society as men's sin was dealt with. The spirit of reconciliation emanating from the Cross was man's ultimate hope, for all who received it were themselves committed to the "ministry of reconciliation" (II Cor. 5:17-20).

"What is redemptive?" is the question which the Christian man must ask if in his life the Cross is to become socially dynamic. This question necessitates that discipline of mind which seeks to understand the issues of an age. But more than this: It requires the cultivation of compassion, and the readiness to identify with the immense and varied suffering of men.

The church is called to share with its Lord His suffering for men (Col. 1:24). It may not have the power to erase all forms of injustice and inhumanity in the world, but it *can* embrace within its heart the suffering of men. It can learn to feel with the outcast, the captive, the despairing. If it cannot of its own power remove the occasions of human agony, the church can choose to *share* that agony in a redemptive way. So may the church become, as Bonhoeffer described it, "a section of humanity in which Christ has taken form."[32]

----

[32]*Ethics*, p. 21; quoted in E. H. Robertson, *Dietrich Bonhoeffer* (Richmond, Va.: John Knox Press, 1967), p. 42.

In its willingness to suffer with the weak and dispossessed, the church becomes free to fulfill its prophetic ministry to the world. Only as it is prepared to become poor will the church be released to serve. Where dependence upon favor or privilege may compromise its freedom, or the desire for security may make it fearful, the willingness to suffer liberates the church. Now it belongs to its Lord — not to some race or class — and it can thus become servant of all.

Faced with imperative decision by the Fugitive Slave Law, amidst the jangling and discord of an age distraught to the point of self-destruction, men desperately needed a *context* of clear thought and undoubted goodwill within which they could engage in the dialogue necessary to understanding and to constructive action. "More light" was, indeed, "wanting somewhere."

But how could the "lonely man of conscience" see the whole, and discover the way out? Solitary man could not in isolation gain the perspective necessary to inform conscience. He needed the *koinonia,* the fellowship of "the community which remembers Jesus," to share insight, to encourage, and to sustain him in the historical moment which demanded decision. He needed the communion of saints to interpret the present crisis in terms of what God had done, and sought to do, to bring in "the new humanity."[33]

But the united, prophetic voice of the Servant-Community was not heard throughout the land. Sectional and sectarian strife weakened the churches' witness in both the South and the North. While some earnestly grappled with the complexities of obedience to a law they considered "unjust," countless others shrugged off any responsibility on the ground that it was a purely political problem. Meanwhile, appeals to "higher laws" confused the sincere, and obscured the one law which is the fountainhead of all justice — "do what love requires,"

---

[33]For a discussion of *"koinonia* ethics" see Paul L. Lehmann, *Ethics In a Christian Context* (New York: Harper and Row, 1963), 45 ff.

But love was deemed anemic and impractical. Instead, men were to appeal to arms. Some even professed to see the regnant Christ "in the watchfires of a hundred circling camps." A holocaust of death and destruction was visited upon the nation — a bloody conflict of "higher laws."

In the name of "conscience" brother was set against brother, each marching to war convinced of the rightness of his cause. The Servant-Community was itself caught up in the maelstrom despite the earnest voices of some who pled that the church should follow peace.

When at last it was finished, the fugitive could no longer be returned to his master. He had no master.

But where was his brother?

VI THE DAY OF VISITATION

Woe unto them that decree unrighteousness decrees . . . What will ye do in the day of visitation . . . ?
— Isaiah 10:1, 3, KJV

It is a shocking experience when the Word of God leaps from the pages of the Bible to confront a man in his daily life. The prophetic Word has a way of arresting one and demanding that he become involved with the issues of the day. For its part, the academic world has long sought meaning through detachment and objectivity. It is a significant judgment upon our educational system that when a question is called "purely academic," one usually means that, although it may be interesting, it is irrelevant.

In their quest for meaning historians and philosophers have suggested various theories to explain the rise and fall of civilizations. The "key" to history has been sought in materialistic necessity, response to challenge, comparing the course of civilization to the blooming and fading of a flower, and in many other motifs. While students have found these theories stimulating and useful for understanding the past, all too many have been content to treat the quest for meaning as "purely academic." After all, who can *prove* whether it is Marx, or Toynbee, or Spengler who is right? Only time will tell.

Yes, time *will* tell. But meanwhile, there are decisions to make and things to do. If the question of meaning can only be *proven* at the end, man must either act without meaning or act in faith. For man, the creature of reason, to act without meaning is an ultimate irony. Therefore, the rational man *must act in faith*. To do otherwise is to abdicate his moral responsibility in history. This the prophets thunderously condemn. For them no great issue of the age is "purely academic."

With one voice the Scriptures declare that God is present in history. He *visits* His people and the nations of the world in their times of critical decision. His presence is as that of a shepherd carrying both "rod and staff" — to bless or to judge. The decision of man determines which it will be.

If many in a scientifically oriented age find it difficult to accept such an assertion, let it be noted that they are in good Biblical company. Long ago the psalmist asked, "What is man, that thou art mindful of him? and the son of man, that thou visitest him?" (Ps. 8:4, KJV). The psalmist freely confesses his wonder as he contemplates the "day of visitation." But because it is a mystery it is not the less true.

To those who seek the will of God, the "day of visitation" brings hope. "Visit me with thy salvation," prays the psalmist (Ps. 106:4). Contemplating the birth of Jesus, the devout Zacharias said, "Blessed be the Lord God of Israel; for he hath visited and redeemed his people" (Luke 1:68, KJV). Viewing the miracle at Nain, in which Jesus restored to life the son of a widow, the rejoicing villagers declared, "God hath visited his people" (Luke 7:16).

But to a generation disobedient to the will of God, the "day of visitation" is judgment. Isaiah speaks of divine judgment upon a "rebellious people" who say to the seers and prophets, "Get you out of the way" (Isa. 30:9-14). To a culture saturated with gross social injustice and religious hypocrisy Amos declares, "And in all vineyards shall be wailing: for I will pass through thee, saith the Lord. Woe unto you that desire the day of the Lord! to what end is it for you? the day of the Lord is darkness, and not light" (Amos 5:17-20, KJV).

But if the prophets condemned Israel of old for disobedience to the divine Presence in history, Jesus wept because the generation to which He came did not recognize their "day of visitation" (Luke 19:44). Ignorance was no less tragic than disobedience.

While some theories of history view man as a helpless pawn acting out a predetermined role, or adrift on some inevitable "wave of the future," it is not so with the prophets. Man cannot "deal himself out" or "beg the question" by withholding historical decision on some fatalistic ground.

Rather, it is given to man to see through the course of events the "footprints of God," who still visits His people to call them to responsible action.[1] To "do justice" and to "love mercy" are His unchanging mandates by which every generation is judged.

The New Testament Scriptures declare that in Christ the end of history is revealed, but men art called by grace to share in its realization. *Man's decision in history is required to fulfill its end.* For this he is responsible.[2]

This means that what modern Americans, white or black, *decide* about such issues as racial justice will in large measure determine the future of this civilization.

Those who lived in the shadow of the Civil War had good cause to appreciate the prophetic declaration that "the Day of the Lord is darkness, not light." The lives of countless common people were visited with confusion, suffering, and death. The sheer difficulty of finding the good to choose amidst the jangling conflicts of loyalties and interests, pressed heavily upon those who would follow conscience.

John Fee, founder of Berea College, who had spoken so forthrightly against the slavery system, was driven from

---

[1]Th. C. Vriezen, *An Outline of Old Testament Theology* (Newton Centre: Charles T. Branford, 1966), p. 57 f.

[2]See Carl Michalson, *The Hinge of History*, (New York: Scribner's, 1959).

ntucky together with his family and close friends.[3] At
the same time, Garfield, then a member of the Ohio Legislature, led in the attempt to heal the growing breach between
the states by helping to host the legislatures of Kentucky
and Tennessee at a banquet in Cincinnati. Fee arrived
penniless — an outcast from the same society which Garfield and his associates were courting.

The irony of this situation was too much for an abolitionist supporter of Garfield who wrote a letter upon which
the future President inscribed, "Read and preserve." In
eloquent language she spoke of the high hopes which many
had held for his gifts. They had seen him as a young "David" who was prepared to strike mighty blows against the
ramparts of bondage. Now his armor was tarnished and the
integrity of his convictions questioned. At the very moment
that Fee and his band of exiles sought refuge in Cincinnati,
Garfield was sharing festivities with the southern legislators
and muttering "sickly sentiments" about the Federal Union.
Carman asked, "How did you thus uncrown yourself?"

Eloquently she declared:

> I believe that God rules, and that the strong
> holds of oppression shall be broken, and earth's en-
> slaved millions shout the anthem of deliverance . . .

---

[3]Fee had been invited by Henry Ward Beecher to speak in Ply-
mouth Church, Brooklyn, at the time of the John Brown raid at Harper's Ferry (October, 1859). In the course of his address he said:
> "We want more John Browns; not in manner of action,
> but in spirit of consecration; not to go with carnal weapons,
> but with spiritual; men who, with Bibles in their hands, and
> tears in their eyes, will beseech men to be reconciled to God.
> Give us such men, and we may yet save the South." Fee,
> *Autobiography*, p. 147.

Upon returning to Kentucky, Fee found that his remark, "We want
more John Browns," was taken from context, which gave it a different
meaning from the original. He was consequently waited on by a
committee of sixty-five of the "most respectable" citizens and given
ten days to leave the state. This ultimatum was given on December
23, 1859. Fee appealed to the Governor, who refused to intervene.
Thus he and others, including John Rogers, principal of Berea, fled
to Cincinnati. *Ibid.*, p. 147.

and yet I sorrow to see talents such as you possess withheld from the cause of human freedom — and that your eloquent voice is heard in the revels of those who fawn on tyrants, and do their will.

The good can well afford to wait the true verdict of time, and though the consummation so wished by all the true and good may be long delayed, yet so sure as God's law is changeless, it will come, and woe to him by whom it is hindered.[4]

On April 12, 1861, the guns of South Carolina opened fire upon Fort Sumter. With the outbreak of hostilities, Virginia, Arkansas, Tennessee, and North Carolina joined the Confederacy. The Civil War had begun.

The outbreak of hostilities cast a dark shadow over Bethany College. Although Campbell had warned the Virginia Constitutional Convention in 1832 that slavery would ultimately blast the nation unless steps were taken in time to eradicate it, he was himself broken to see the fulfillment of his own prophecy. With the news of war the college was temporarily closed, and the students scattered. The "riot" of 1855 was still vivid in Campbell's mind.[5] Now the worst had happened.

Garfield visited Bethany in June, 1861. He found Campbell but a shadow of his former self. Like so many families in the border states, his was divided in its loyalties. Campbell was true to the Union, but his son, wife, and daughter

---

[4]James A. Garfield Papers, 1860, no. 127.

[5]This disturbance had arisen among students of the college over the slavery issue. The students who had left had been received as heroes in Indianapolis, and became the first class of North-Western Christian University (now Butler). Not content with this, they had written of Campbell, "We believe he has made an impression upon the world, which the trembling hand of age will not have strength enough to deepen, although it may avail . . . to dim and mar its beauty." The Bethany faculty had angrily responded to this unnecessary slur. *Millennial Harbinger*, (1856), pp. 57 f., 169-173, 228. *Weekly State Journal*, January 17, 1856. (This paper was edited by B. R. Sulgrove, and published in Indianapolis. Ovid Butler had financial interest in the *Journal*.)

sympathized with the South. "It is sad to see a family so divided," Garfield wrote to a friend. Mournfully Campbell frequently remarked, "I shall never see peace in this country again."[6] Even so, amidst the evidences of divine judgment, Campbell's faith asserted itself. In 1865, toward the end of the ordeal, he was to write his last essay for the *Harbinger* on the text, "Behold I will create all things new!"[7]

As a people which had pled for Christian unity, the Disciples now found themselves divided politically. What would they do in that "day of visitation?" Many of them rushed to arms, but not all.

Campbell had for years opposed war and his influence had been felt among the churches. In an "Address on War" delivered in Wheeling in 1848 he had declared, "War is not now, nor was it ever, a process of justice." It was in no sense "a test of truth — a criterion of right."[8] In June, 1861, he wrote again, calling war the "climax of human folly." Civil war was yet worse. That a nation "boasting of a humane and Christian paternity and fraternity" should unsheath the sword and shed fraternal blood, was to him "the climax of all human inconsistencies inscribed on the blurred and moth eaten pages of time in all its records."[9]

In this conviction Campbell was joined by other leaders. The evangelist, Benjamin Franklin, wrote, "We will not take up arms against, fight and kill the brethren we have labored for twenty years to bring into the kingdom of God."[10] From Canada David Oliphant wrote, "We trust that disciples of the high and hallowed Prince, whose government 'is righteousness, peace, and joy in the Holy Spirit' — a

---

[6]Garfield to Harmon Austin (a trustee of Hiram College), in Theodore C. Smith, *Life and Letters of James Abram Garfield* (2 vols., New Haven, 1925), I, p. 166.

[7]Robert Richardson, *Memoirs of Alexander Campbell* (2 vols., Cincinnati, 1897), II, p. 655.

[8]*Millennial Harbinger,* (1848), p. 361 f.

[9]*Ibid.,* (1861), p. 348.

[10]*American Christian Review*, in Garrison and DeGroot, *Disciples of Christ*, p. 335.

government established to save and not destroy — will stand aloof from such a godless contest and destructive strife."[11]

Thomas Munnell, debating the eminent preacher, J. S. Sweeney, blamed the "preachers from New Orleans to Boston" for so inflaming the prejudices of people that now they were being led "like swine to the slaughter." He firmly believed that if the Christians of America had refused to go to war, there would have been no such conflict.[12]

James A. Butler saw in the threat of war a tremendous opportunity for the church. A month before the fall of Sumter he wrote, "This is a favorable time to plead the Gospel as the power of God, and the unity of the church as an item of this power." From the time man first committed murder human wisdom had "proved a failure." Surely, such a crisis as faced the nation would turn men to God![13]

Writing from Nashville in the same month, David Lipscomb said, "In the mad excitement of the hour" a person might feel constrained to "cut loose from every sacred obligation," and join "the wild senseless rush of men who take counsel of their passions rather than their reason." He knew that many felt the words of "the humble peace-loving Nazarene" were not for such times. They spoke of "war and butchery" with delight, as if such things were the "fruits of the spirit." To Lipscomb it was clear that "violence of every order" was forbidden by the New Testament. "God's kingdom is a kingdom of peace," he wrote, "and its subjects are men of peace."[14]

From Missouri, John R. Howard wrote, "Our religion is one of LOVE." If Christians were actuated by love, they would of necessity oppose all war. To those who protested that this would leave the nation defenseless, Howard re-

---

[11]*Banner of the Faith*, XV (1861), p. 105. Edited by David Oliphant and others (Hamilton, Ontario, 1846-1864?). This periodical was "moderate" on the slavery issue.

[12]Thomas Munnell, and J. S. Sweeney, *Shall Christians Go to War?* (Cincinnati, 1872), pp. 172, 173.

[13]*Gospel Advocate*, VII (1861), p. 88.

[14]*Ibid.*, VII (1861), pp. 82, 83.

plied that the very question was "a virtual renunciation of
confidence in the protection of God!" However, if any man
believed that he could enlist in the struggle and one day receive the approval of God, he was "at liberty" to do so.[15]

As if in direct answer to the prophet's question, "What
will ye do in the day of visitation?" John W. McGarvey led
a number of preachers from Missouri to circularize a declaration throughout the nation. McGarvey had posed the
question to the churches:

> Brethren at the North and at the South what say
> you? Shall we be able, when this war is over, to
> meet each other in council again, and be able to say
> that not one Christian has enlisted in the armies, or
> fallen in the field, by the consent of any one of us?
> That we have warned and entreated all to pursue
> the things that make for peace, and are free from
> the blood of all men?[16]

It is significant that the most courageous answer to this
question came from Missouri, a border state where soldiers
of both sides learned to live off the land, and where "bush-
whackers" murdered and terrified a helpless populace. Four-
teen preachers of Missouri expressed their daring vision of
the church in a "Circular." During a time when the churches
were tempted to reflect the bitterness of sectional strife the
"Circular" called for Christians to be true to their Lord. Let
the churches mold the social order instead of being molded
by it! They dared to declare that "a body of Disciples so
closely bound by the word of God alone that not even the
shock of civil war" could divide them, would prove a great
power in the ultimate healing of the nation.[17]

---

[15]*Christian Pioneer*, I (1861), pp. 17, 18, 127, 142. This periodical
was edited by John Howard and others, (Lindley; Trenton; Chilli-
clothe, Mo., 1861-1870).

[16]*Ibid.*, I (1861), pp. 169, 170.

[17]*American Christian Review* in *Christian Pioneer*, I (1861), pp.
181, 182. Signatories to the circular were B. H. Smith, T. M.
Allen, J. J. Errett, E. V. Rice, J. K. Rogers, J. D. Dawson, J. Atkin-
son, J. W. Cox, Samuel Johnson, R. C. Morton, H. H. Haley, T.
P. Haley, Levi Van Camp, J. W. McGarvey.

In October, 1861, the annual meeting of the American Christian Missionary Society was held in Cincinnati. Many of the brethren could not attend from south of the Ohio because of military operations. Even so, affirmations of continuing unity came to the gathering. From Lexington, George W. Elley wrote:

> May God grant to you, and the whole brotherhood, a strong faith, an ardent love for him and the whole house of his Israel. May your meeting demonstrate that we are yet one, that the "unity of the spirit in the bonds of love," can and shall be maintained. May Satan's effort to divide us into sections be overruled; and may the gospel of our salvation triumph over all opposing foes.
>
> Now is the day of our trial, and this is the day of our triumph. — "Watch ye, stand fast in the faith, quit you like men; let your things be done with love."[18]

Perhaps it was too much to expect that such a gathering could altogether rise above the conflict which so engrossed the nation. Some were concerned lest the appeals to "follow the things which make for peace" would be interpreted as disloyalty to the Union. They seemed not to understand that those in the South who took the antiwar position were subject to the same accusation with reference to the Confederacy. Feelings were running high, however, and Dr. J. P. Robinson of Ohio introduced a "Loyalty Resolution" into the assembly. Because it was ruled not germane to the business of a missionary gathering, a recess was declared and the same men, as a mass meeting, passed the resolution. Garfield, wearing the uniform of a colonel, spoke in its behalf. Although it was passed "unanimously," a large number refused to vote, including Campbell himself.[19]

---

[18]*Minutes, American Christian Missionary Society,* (1861), pp. 38, 39.

[19]*Ibid.,* (1861), p. 20.

So the nation appealed to arms. Whether slavery was the primary cause of the war has long been debated by historians. Whatever may be their ultimate verdict, it is true that countless thousands marched in the name of "freedom."

The South fought for a way of life which was admittedly based on slavery, but which preserved the values of sectional determination. The North fought in the name of freeing the slave, and to preserve the Union. So the holocaust was "justified" on both sides.

It is difficult for a modern to appreciate the terrible cost of the Civil War. The figures are there: the North lost in dead, 359,528, and in wounded, 275,175. The South lost 258,000 dead, and over 100,000 wounded. Perhaps these figures take on more meaning when we note that approximately one Union soldier died for each slave in Louisiana, and one Confederate soldier died for each slave in Kentucky. In all, there were just under four million slaves in 1860 who were liberated by the war.[20]

Or were they?

Did the appeal to violence solve the *fundamental* problem which white and black in America face? We have noted how the slave members of the Pleasant Grove, Kentucky, congregation requested in 1854 that they be permitted to segregate themselves. It will be remembered that the white members of the church refused the request.[21] After the war the record would read differently. In 1868, on a page which speaks with silent eloquence, the Clerk, John W. Williamson, inscribed in red ink the following:

> All that you see written in Red is an emblem of the distressed condition of our country and the great flow of Blood spilt caurlessly in our land from 1860 to 1865.

---

[20]See *Encyclopedia of American History*, ed. by Richard B. Morriss (New York: Harper & Bros., 1953), p. 516.

[21]*Supra*, p. 72.

Williamson then inscribed the following minute:

> On the 15th day of Augt. 1868 after worship Brother Hoke preached we then proceeded to revise our church book we found that our total number was 28 members 4 males and 24 females.
>
> is ordered that all the church colloured members be excluded they all having left in disorder.[22]

So began the segregation of those churches which had long retained slave and master in one congregational life. Freedom from one's former master meant freedom from his leadership in the church as well. Some slaves who had been baptized by whites were rebaptized by members of their own race.[23] The spirit of alienation ran high in many places. In retrospect, Tolbert Fanning wrote:

> Time was when thousands of the best informed colored people of the south lived in full fellowship as members of the church of Christ, with their white brethren. They prayed, sang, exhorted and broke bread together, as members of one family. . . . These people sat with their white brethren many years in heavenly places in Christ Jesus. It was a joyful season. Our colored brethren, some of whom at least we aided in purchasing and setting at liberty, and others whom we had educated in what seemed to us, useful and good, without our agency, were completely alienated from us, and turned against us. The revolution was too sudden and too great, for the moral health of the freed people. They were induced to think, that all with whom they had formerly associated, were oppressive, and enemies of the colored race. Such seems to be the general opinion still.[24]

In North Carolina, the Concord Church at Pantego segregated by the following action:

---

[22]Pleasant Grove Minutes, August 15, 1868.

[23]M. F. Harmon, *A History of the Christian Churches in Mississippi* (Aberdeen: 1929), p. 112.

[24]"The Colored People of the South" in *The Religious Historian* Tolbert Fanning, ed. (Nashville, Tenn.), I (1872), pp. 89, 90.

First Lord's Day in Feb. 1868

On motion agreed that the following named persons have a letter of dismission to form a new Church viz:

Luke Gurganus	Kiziah Flynn
Sarah Gaylord	Sylvia Wilkinson
Lucy Johnson	Miriam Clark
Maria Tyson	Anna Clark
Marg t Flynn	Matilda Eborn
Emily Campbell	Hutchins Windley
Margaret Whitley	Matilda Swindell
Rebecca Swindell	Joseph Whitley

The clerk will give them a letter of dismission.[25]

There is nothing in this minute to indicate the act to be anything unusual. Were one not familiar with the names of slaves in the congregation through perusal of former minutes, there would be no way of knowing that this was in fact an act of segregation. Here the former slaves were quietly released to "form a new church."

This procedure was in accord with that of the Annual State Meeting of the Christian churches of North Carolina in 1868. There the following motion was passed:

> Resolved, That we recommend to the churches composing this Conference, that where they have a sufficient number of colored members to form an independent organization, they allow them to do so, if they desire it, by giving them letters of dismission for that purpose. That we deeply sympathize with the colored people with reference to their spiritual welfare, and that we willingly teach them the gospel of Christ in its purity as opportunity admits.[26]

At the Annual Meeting of 1869 the following further action was taken:

---

[25]Pantego Minutes.
[26]Charles C. Ware, *North Carolina Disciples of Christ* (St. Louis, 1927), p. 224.

> That the colored brethren be advised to form a separate conference, and that Elders A. J. Battle, H. D. Cason, J. R. Winfield, Henry Gurganus, and R. J. T. Walsh be appointed to confer with, and assist them in their organization.

The Minutes of the Annual Meeting of 1870 record:

> Having heard with pleasure that the colored disciples have partially at least succeeded in organizing their Conference, we bid them God speed.[27]

The break was not complete, however, for at the second Annual Meeting of Colored Disciples, in 1873, white preachers were present. The *Watch Tower* reported the gathering as follows:

> Before dispersing, the white preachers went forward to the public stand and gave the hand of fellowship and brotherly recognition to the colored ministers present — an example that was followed by several private members of high social position who were among the audience. The effect on the colored people was good — and will settle them more firmly in the faith.[28]

From this standpoint it is not difficult to see that even in his good intentions the *Watch Tower* reporter betrayed that patronizing feeling which is so offensive to modern Blacks, and has rather served to *"unsettle* them in the faith."

Perhaps it was to be expected that so long as black and white sustained the slave-master relationship, their fellowship in the church would be characterized by white domination. The church lived in the world, and could hardly be insulated completely from the social mores of the time. Meanwhile, the leadership abilities of the slaves remained largely undeveloped because of restrictions upon their education.

The Negro church had found its most early development

---

[27]*Ibid.,* p. 225.
[28]*Ibid.,* p. 226.

in the period of the American Revolution largely due to
white prejudice.[29] But among the Christian Churches and
Churches of Christ the quest of Christian unity had constrained black and white to worship together. Yet, even
here, the unity was incomplete, for where the church does
not challenge the inequities of the social order those inequities will compromise the fellowship of the church.

Under conditions granting the utmost sympathy and goodwill, the ever present white leadership subtly conditioned
the religious freedom of the Black. Somehow he needed to
be free to express himself in leadership through those cultural forms meaningful to himself. The principle of the in-
digenous church so lately recognized on the "mission field"
was here relevant, but not adequately appreciated.

While racial segregation has often been expressive of
prejudice and ill will, *it is not always so.* The black separation for worship was, at least in part, *a quest for authenticity.* In terms of contemporary church life this means that
"integration" at the expense of authenticity is no true solution. At the same time, however, authenticity in Christ is
not fulfilled through *separation* from a brother.

The solution will only be found in a genuine sharing of
common life like that reflected in the New Testament in
which diversity of cultural response to the Word of God is
seen as an enrichment of faith, and as a valued treasure of
"the communion of saints."

Though the fellowship of master and slave in a common
congregational life was conditioned by their social relationship, was the segregation which followed any better? Does
a broken fellowship more adequately express the kingdom
of God than an imperfect one? Cultural separation even in
the name of authenticity cannot be accepted as the final

---

[29]Winthrop D. Jordan has traced the early schism which led to
the development of the first Negro churches in Philadelphia, saying,
"It meant that the one institution which was at all prepared to accept
the Negro as an equal was shattered." *White Over Black* (Baltimore:
Pelican Books, 1969), p. 425.

form of the church, for separation leads to ignorance, and ignorance is the fertile seedbed of prejudice.

The one institution which was in any way prepared to sustain a viable relationship between white and black was shattered. This was perhaps the most tragic development to follow the Civil War.[30] The freedman's right to "pick up and go" included the right to leave churches which even under the best intentions were dominated by their former masters. Yet this separation has had profound implications, as is seen in the attitudes of modern youth.[31] That the Negro church has exerted a powerful influence within the black community is commonly recognized. Indeed, it has long stood as a focal point of Negro life and culture.[32] Meanwhile, the white Protestant church has become increasingly isolated from the Negro community, and in metropolitan areas is largely identified with the white middle class.[33]

The question the Christian must ask is whether the church of Christ is properly to be made an instrument of *any* people's exclusive social or racial identity. Is it in keeping with Christ's will for His church that it become a focus of white or black, middle or lower class identity? How does the good news that Jesus "died for all" justify such a situation?

Gibson Winter succinctly states the question this way: "How can an inclusive message be mediated through an exclusive group, when the principle of exclusiveness is social-class identity rather than a gift of faith which is open to all?"[34]

---

[30]C. Vann Woodward, *The Strange Career of Jim Crow* (Oxford: Oxford University Press, second rev. ed., 1967), p. 22.

[31]E. Franklin Frazier, *Negro Youth at the Crossways* (New York: Schocken Books, 1967), p. 112 f.

[32]E. Franklin Frazier has an excellent discussion of the Negro Church in *The Negro in the United States,* (New York: Macmillan, 1967), chap. xiv.

[33]Gibson Winter, *The Suburban Captivity of the Churches* (New York: Macmillan, 1962), p. 43 f.

[34]*Ibid.,* p. 33.

A new "day of visitation" confronts America, a day
compounded by a multitude of wrongs since the judgment
of the nation in the Civil War. If the North did, indeed,
fight to emancipate the slave, it did not fight to grant the
free Negro status before the law equal to either white native
born or white foreign born. Even before the War, "Black
Laws" restricting the citizenship of free Negroes had been
passed in Indiana, Ohio, Illinois, Michigan, Wisconsin,
Iowa, California, Oregon, Kansas, Massachusetts, New York
and Pennsylvania. The significance of these various acts is
not simply that they were passed, but that they represented
a sentiment widely spread throughout the nation: The Negro's freedom to "pick up and go" did not include the freedom to enter fully the white man's world.[35]

Emancipation did not erase this feeling, but rather ex-
acerbated it. The development of Jim Crow in the South
was accompanied by powerful restrictive racial patterns in
the North and West. The last several decades have seen the
bursting of the dike, and Negro migration out of the South
has become a veritable flood, only now showing signs of
moderating. The cultural shock of this monumental shift of
population is well-nigh immeasurable. Moving from a rural
way of life in the South, multitudes have entered an urban way
of life in the North and West for which they were not prepared.

In the great cities a complex of factors have transformed
once prosperous and beautiful areas into ugly, degenerated
slums often called "ghettos." Ignorance, squalor, poverty
and crime create a vicious whirlpool from which it is difficult to escape. The flight of the middle class, both white
and Negro, from such circumstances simply creates a larger
vacuum into which the squalor and poverty expand. So
the sociological processes of segregation, invasion, and suc-

---

[35]C. Vann Woodward, "White Racism and Black 'Emancipation,'"
in *The New York Review of Books,* Feb. 27, 1969 (New York: The
New York Review, 1969).

cession have revolutionized urban life in America. Although the psychological impact of these developments is difficult to measure it has obviously been profound.

As their members have moved, and removed, in order to escape the expanding black population, white churches have located and relocated in efforts to preserve themselves. To their immense credit, some congregations have remained, making heroic efforts to minister in keeping with the mandate of the Gospel. New forms of ministry and congregational life have appeared. But the way is not easy, for it requires the bridging of a significant cultural and economic gap. It yet remains to be seen whether the institutional life which has become associated with middle class Protestantism is viable in such a radically changing scene.[36]

The law as interpreted by the Supreme Court of the land has declared the right of the black citizen to take up residence in white neighborhoods. But the courts have not restricted the right of the white man to "move out." Thus, segregation has been followed by resegregation, as in the city of Washington. The problem therefore remains, but with this difference: The Black is increasingly disillusioned with the efficacy of law. The law has not solved his problem — at least not as effectively as he had been led to hope. Nor does it appear that the mood of the nation, white or black, betokens an increased dependence upon the rule of law.

If the rule of law is abandoned, there remain two alternatives: embodiment of the love of God in the relation of man to his fellow, or violence. But many are as disillusioned with love as with law. The assassination of Martin Luther King is, for many Blacks, sufficient indication of the inadequacy of love in the face of violence. Therefore, vio-

---

[36]Winter, *op. cit.,* p. 163 f. A significant study of church life in an inner city is found in Gerald D. Suttles, *The Social Order of the Slum* (Chicago: University of Chicago Press, 1968), p. 41 f. See also the eloquent appeal of William E. Pannell in *My Friend, The Enemy* (Waco, Tex.: Word Books, 1968), p. 120 f.

lence is the choice of an increasing number of Blacks, as well
as it is of whites.

It is common for militant members of the black community to assert that what they failed to gain through the
patience and subservience of Booker T. Washington, and
through the legal program of the National Association for
the Advancement of Colored People, they have achieved
through violence. "Whitey" is said to have no respect either
for love or law. It is only through violence that he has been
made to listen. Riots such as those in Watts, Detroit, or
Washington are said to have accomplished more in a few
days than all the legal cases sponsored by the NAACP,
or the ideals of Dr. King and the Negro churches.

Yet, for all its attraction to a disillusioned or desperate
people violence is *no true solution*. What may appear to be
"the only way out" proves historically to be but a mad cycle.
Cultural forms and social institutions which perpetuated
injustice may have been destroyed, but violence will have
sown fresh seeds of hatred and prejudice which are soon
embodied in new forms and institutions. This cycle is succinctly analyzed by Lerone Bennett in four stages:

First is the "original act" of violence, in this case the enslavement of the African, and the establishment of institutions which were developed to keep him in bondage. Emancipation was followed by restrictions which in large measure
continued the original condition.

Second, the group which is oppressed internalizes the
violence which has been done upon it. Its frustrations are
focused upon its own members. (It is significant that while
the crime rate among blacks is higher than the national
norm, the largest percentage of their victims are Blacks.)[37]

The third step takes place when violence returns upon itself in the form of the "oppressed" externalizing their anger

---

[37]*Violent Crime, The Report of the National Commission on the
Causes and Prevention of Violence,* (New York: George Braziller,
1969), pp. 42, 43.

upon the persons or institutions they hold responsible for their plight.

Finally, violence reflected back upon "oppressors" leads to an "intensification of the original violence." So the southern states reacted to Nat Turner's revolt by implementing laws forbidding slave education. In our time the measure of the "white backlash" is as yet unknown, but one may well expect that if the violence of one race enlarges so will the counterviolence of the other.[38]

Unthinkable as it may seem, contemporary America may face another "day of visitation" the consequences of which could make the over half-million dead of the Civil War seem but a prelude. The complexity of the problem is compounded by the sapping of the moral fibre of the nation resulting from its involvement in almost constant warfare for the last two generations. The political use of hysteria makes the situation all the more explosive. Violence increasingly becomes a way of life.

Evil is like the organism which can mutate from one form to another when the first form is threatened with extinction. The trouble is that even those who understand this may in desperation appeal to violence — not because it is "a way out," but because the tormentors must at least be made to suffer with the tormented. Like some Samson, if one must die he will bring down the temple of society upon all. The same desperate mentality which could trigger an atomic holocaust could spark a catastrophic race war.

In the face of such a crisis, the church in America needs to hear its own Scriptures when they say:

> For the time is come that judgment must begin at the house of God: and if it first begin at us, what shall the end be of them that obey not the gospel of God? (I Peter 4:17, KJV).

---

[38]Lerone Bennett, Jr., *Pioneers in Protest* (New York: Penguin Books, 1969), pp. 90, 91.

The church is judged because its members share the social destiny of the world into which it is sent. But more important, it is judged as the steward of the Gospel. The church must answer to its Lord for the way in which it has allowed an unregenerate society to determine the nature of its life and mission. It is inconceivable that the church — white and black — can seriously continue to claim to speak for the Son of Man, and to embody His ministry of reconciliation, while allowing the alienation in the world to sunder its own fellowship. Nor is this sinful situation to be rectified by some artificial "integration" of the churches.

The church is steward of a higher gift than "integration." Its Lord gave it "koinonia" — "fellowship" — the *sharing of a common life*. It is quite possible for a congregation to be "integrated" while having no true *communion* of life with life.

While the church is not called to force its will upon the social order, it is required by its Lord *to exemplify in its way of life what the kingdom of God is*. Were it to do this the impact upon society would be profound. But the church's *failure* to do this is evidenced in the hosts of disillusioned youth of the land. But irrespective of whether society will behold or receive the Kingdom, the church is obliged to demonstrate in its common life of faith, hope, and charity that which God seeks for all men.

What this means in terms of American church life may yet remain to be seen. But the principles and example of such a way are to be found in the church of the first century, whose record is in the New Testament. The church must therefore seek renewal through recovery of that primitive faith, spirit, and fellowship. It needs to recover for its institutions the elasticity and diversity which characterized early Christianity, in which *mission* and *movement* were paramount. The church must learn to depend utterly upon its Lord, and to speak His word with boldness, while embodying in its life the miracle of transforming love.

The church must learn afresh that the identity which

men find in Christ is to transcend every other form of social identity. Whatever must be done to *realize* this — to translate it from doctrine into life — must be done. In many places this will necessitate a vision of the church which has risen above the "chumminess" of like-situated people, and dares to gather within itself, as in the beginning, the diversity of the world brought to the feet of Jesus.

The church must learn again to believe in the power of love, and *to submit itself to that power*. It must be willing to embody that love, with all its hurt and cost, where its Lord embodied it in the marketplaces and crossroads of the world. The church must learn afresh that the same Lord who calls it together *sends it forth* to become involved person to person in men's lostness, that they might find salvation.

The church must cease being concerned with generalities, and become concerned for persons. Rather than wringing its hands over the mighty power which hatred and prejudice wield, it should see that power as a multiplication of ten thousand individual acts of hatred and prejudice which have permeated the social order. *Only from a distance* do these individual acts appear one massive force. Since evil is not general, a "generalized love" cannot come to grips with it. *It is the failure of "love in general" to meet the myriad evil acts of men which has disillusioned so many with the power of love.*

The church is called to counter the massive multiplication of evil deeds by a myriad of loving acts which meet hatred and prejudice on their own ground. So the Cross becomes more than an event of past history, and more than a principle — it becomes a dynamic way of living daily. God does not love the world in general, but *in particular* — each man, whether prodigal, Samaritan or publican. The church must learn again what it is to love in this way.

The love of which we speak is not weak sentimentality. Neither is it satisfied with "token" acts (such as requiring every denominational board to have a black member). It speaks the truth to the white man, calling him to examine his own actions and attitudes in light of the mandate to love one's neighbor as one's self. It speaks truth to the black man, willing to recognize the complexities of his problems, but challenging him not to use his disadvantages as an excuse for not achieving what he can. It calmly asks the white man whether he would tolerate conditions such as are imposed upon many Blacks. It calls upon the black man not to stereotype whites into "Whitey" any more than he wants to be stereotyped. It requires the white man not to be content to receive those blessings which come to him because of his color so long as his black neighbor is refused such opportunities because of his color. It urges patience upon the white man when the Black tends to overcompensate in some newly-found freedom. It teaches the black and white alike that one's own sense of self-respect will be manifested by respect for others. These are the practical, hard tasks which love alone can do. By their very nature law or violence can never accomplish these things.

Love is openness to another person in giving and receiving. Love demands justice of custom, law, and institutions. Love is tough-fibered, courageous, persistent.

This love is *intelligence disciplined for the good of another*. In a day of popularized prejudice and cynicism love dares to bear, believe, hope, endure, give.

This is the love which the church is called to embody.

As did the fathers, so has this generation "eaten sour grapes"; and as we have found our "teeth on edge," so will our children. Unless — (is the word too small for the magnitude of the alternative?) — unless this generation succeeds in interdicting the fateful sequence by a decisive act of repentance and reconciliation.

A century ago the ex-slave, Frederick Douglass was to write:

> We are here, and here we are likely to be. To imagine that we should ever be eradicated is absurd and ridiculous. We can be modified, changed, assimi-

lated, but never extinguished. We repeat, therefore, that we are here; and this is our country; and the question for the philosophers and statesmen of the land ought to be, What principle should dictate the policy of the nation toward us? We shall neither die out, nor be driven out; but shall go with this people, either as a testimony against them, or as an evidence in their favor throughout their generation. . . .[39]

What will ye do in the day of visitation?

Do What Love Requires.

---

[39]*Ibid.,* p. 209.